SIZZLE IT

140 TASTY GRILL RECIPES

ABOUT WEIGHT WATCHERS

Weight Watchers International, Inc. is the world's leading provider of weight management services, operating globally through a network of Company-owned and franchise operations. Weight Watchers holds over 48,000 weekly meetings, where members receive group support and education about healthful eating patterns, behavior modification, and physical activity. Weight-loss and weight-management results vary by individual. We recommend that you attend Weight Watchers meetings to benefit from the supportive environment you'll find there and follow the comprehensive Weight Watchers program, which includes food plans, an activity plan, and a thinking-skills plan. In addition, Weight Watchers offers a wide range of products, publications and programs for those interested in weight loss and weight control. For the Weight Watchers meeting nearest you, call **800-651-6000.** For information on bringing Weight Watchers to your workplace, call **800-8AT-WORK.** Also, visit us at our Web site, **WeightWatchers.com,** or look for *Weight Watchers Magazine* at your newsstand or in your meeting room.

GINGER CHICKEN YAKITORI,
PAGE 27

WEIGHT WATCHERS PUBLISHING GROUP

EDITORIAL DIRECTOR	NANCY GAGLIARDI
CREATIVE DIRECTOR	ED MELNITSKY
PRODUCTION MANAGER	ALAN BIEDERMAN
OFFICE MANAGER AND PUBLISHING ASSISTANT	JENNY LABOY-BRACE
FOOD EDITOR	EILEEN RUNYAN
EDITOR	DEBORAH MINTCHEFF
NUTRITION CONSULTANT	U. BEATE KRINKE
RECIPE DEVELOPERS	LORI LONGBOTHAM MAUREEN LUCHEJKO JACKIE MILLS SARAH REYNOLDS
PHOTOGRAPHER	JAMES BAIGRIE
FOOD STYLIST	MICHAEL PEDERSON
PROP STYLIST	CATHY COOK
ART DIRECTOR	LISA CUMMINGS
DESIGNER & ILLUSTRATOR	DANIELA HRITCU

ON THE COVER: Maple-Brined Pork Chops with Basil-Stuffed Nectarines (**POINTS**® value: **6**), page 96

ABOUT OUR RECIPES

We make every effort to ensure that you will have success with our recipes. For best results and for nutritional accuracy, please keep the following guidelines in mind:

- Recipes in this book have been developed for Weight Watchers members who are following either the **Flex Plan** or the **Core Plan**® on **TurnAround.**® All **Core Plan** recipes are marked with our **Core Plan** recipe icon ☑. We include **POINTS**® values so you can use any of the recipes if you are following the **Flex Plan** on the program. **POINTS** values are assigned based on calories, fat (grams), and fiber (grams) provided for a serving size of a recipe.

- All recipes feature approximate nutritional information; our recipes are analyzed for Calories (Cal), Total Fat (Fat), Saturated Fat (Sat Fat), Trans Fat (Trans Fat), Cholesterol (Chol), Sodium (Sod), Carbohydrates (Carb), Dietary Fiber (Fib), Protein (Prot), and Calcium (Calc).

- Nutritional information for recipes that include meat, poultry, and fish are based on cooked skinless boneless portions (unless otherwise stated), with the fat trimmed.

- We recommend that you buy lean meat and poultry, then trim it of all visible fat before cooking. When poultry is cooked with the skin on, we suggest removing the skin before eating.

- We follow the USDA guidelines for cooking meats and poultry to safe temperatures to prevent foodborne illness, but for beef and lamb (steaks, roasts, and chops) be aware that cooking them to the recommended minimum of 145°F will give you a medium-cooked steak, roast, or chop.

- Before serving, divide foods—including vegetables, sauce, or accompaniments—into portions of equal size according to the designated number of servings per recipe.

- Any substitutions made to the ingredients will alter the "Per serving" nutritional information and may affect the **Core Plan** recipe status or the **POINTS** value.

- All fresh fruits, vegetables, and greens in recipes should be rinsed before using.

MOJITO-BARBECUED CHICKEN,
PAGE 65, AND MEXICAN
GRILLED CORN, PAGE 142

CONTENTS

HOW TO GRILL
guide

Pick a Grill
Match a grill to your grilling style

The Right Stuff
Choose the tools that will have you grilling like a pro

Firing up the Grill
What you need to get a fire going

Grill Temperature Know-How
How to get the most accurate temperature from your grill

Direct & Indirect Grilling
All you need to know about these two basic grilling techniques

Flavoring the Fire
Easy ways to add tempting flavor to grilled food

Grilling Safety
Common-sense advice for safe grilling

Time/Temperature Chart
All the information you need to grill food to perfection

GETTING STARTED

Firing up the grill on the weekend is as American as apple pie and state fairs. And whether you grill on one of the latest state-of-the-art stainless-steel models or a simple kettle-type grill, the pleasure derived from eating a juicy grilled steak or plump piece of chicken is equally satisfying.

What follows is all you need to know to grill easily and safely: the various types of grills, how to light and flavor the fire, and how to tell how hot the fire is. As an added bonus, we've included an easy-to-follow chart that gives the grilling time and doneness temperatures for various cuts of beef, pork, and lamb, as well as for poultry and fish.

PICK A GRILL

Looking to buy a grill? The good news is that you don't need to spend a lot of money to purchase a good-quality piece of equipment. Here's the lowdown on the kinds of grills available to match your grilling style.

- **Gas Grills** the number-one top sellers, are for cooks who prefer the convenience of quick-starting ignition and minimal cleanup. Gas grills are available with a variety of options, including two or more burners, electric ignition, fuel gauge, warming racks, and storage cabinets.

- **Charcoal Grills** appeal to grilling enthusiasts who enjoy the ritual of igniting charcoal briquettes or natural hardwood charcoal. The simplest model is the Japanese-style hibachi, a small cast-iron grill that is just right for a small patio. For more ambitious grilling, choose a large covered kettle-type grill. Or choose a brazier, a midsize uncovered grill. Some charcoal grills are available with gas ignition, which lights the charcoal with the press of a button.

- **Electric-Style Gas Grills**, often less expensive than gas grills, have artificial briquettes that produce an authentically smoky flavor. There are large electric grills for the backyard, as well as tabletop models.

THE RIGHT STUFF

These handy, helpful tools will have you grilling like a pro:

- **Silicone Basting Brush** Burned bristles are a thing of the past thanks to heatproof silicone brushes. Look for an extra-long, angled handle to keep you from getting burned when reaching for food at the back of the grill.

- **Brass-Bristled Scrub Brush** This heavy-duty, rust-resistant brush is designed to clean a grill rack.

- **Grill Basket** A good option for delicate or small foods, grilling baskets come in various shapes. There are fish-shaped baskets for whole fish, as well as square and oblong baskets with handles.

- **Grill Mitts** These are longer than standard oven mitts to protect more of your arms, and they are better insulated to protect you from the intense heat of the grill.

- **Instant-read Thermometer** Insert this thermometer into grilled food and the dial gives you a reading in seconds. Choose one with a large easy-to-read dial. Some models light up for after-dark grilling.

- **Long-Handled Kitchen Tongs** These make turning food easy. Unlike a fork, they don't puncture the food, which causes the flavorful juices to escape. Look for stainless-steel tongs with silicone-coated tips.

- **Lump Hardwood Charcoal** If you own a charcoal grill, nothing delivers smoky, hearty barbecue flavor better than 100 percent all-natural lump hardwood charcoal. It is available in supermarkets and in large hardware stores.

- **Skewers** Long metal skewers are a must for kebabs. Choose skewers with flat shafts, which prevent the food from slipping around. Or use wooden skewers, but be sure to soak them in water for 30 minutes. A great new option are double metal skewers that have a long U-shape. The food is threaded through both prongs, which prevents the food from spinning when turned.

- **Spatula** Use a spatula with a long, heatproof handle for flipping burgers and moving food on a grill topper (see below).

- **Spray Bottle/Mister** Fill a spray bottle with water and keep it on hand. At the first sign of a flare-up, move the food to a cooler portion of the grill and douse the flames.

- **Vegetable Grill Topper (Grid)** This perforated metal sheet or mesh screen allows you to grill small items, such as vegetables or shrimp, that would otherwise fall through the grill rack.

FIRING UP THE GRILL

Here's what you need to know to get the fire going:

GAS AND ELECTRIC GRILLS are a cinch to light. Just follow the manufacturer's directions for turning on the burners.

CHARCOAL GRILLS require a little more work: Spread an even layer of charcoal briquettes over the bottom of the firebox, then stack them in a pyramid. Use one of the following methods to get the fire started with ease:

- **Electric Starter** Place this device, a loop-shaped heating element with a handle, in a bed of charcoal briquettes and plug it into an electric outlet. Once the coals are ashed over, which will take about 15 minutes, remove the starter.

- **Solid Fire Starters** These nontoxic waxy-looking cubes light easily. Place them on the bottom of the grill, light them, and place the charcoal on top. They burn steadily even when wet.

- **Chimney Starter** This is an open-ended metal cylinder with a handle. Place the starter on the grill. Place a few sheets of crumpled newspaper in the bottom of the cylinder and top with briquettes. Light the newspaper through one of the holes in the cylinder and wait until the coals are covered with gray ash, about 20 minutes. Dump the lit charcoal into the bottom of the grill and spread the coals to form an even layer.

GRILL TEMPERATURE KNOW-HOW

A charcoal fire is just the right temperature when the coals are about 80 percent ashed over (covered with gray ash). Double-check the temperature using this method:

Take the Test Hold an outstretched palm 4 to 5 inches above the coals. The length of time you can stand the heat indicates the temperature of the grill.

Time	Heat
2 seconds	**Hot**
3–4 seconds	**Medium-high**
5–6 seconds	**Medium**
7 seconds	**Low**

Adjust the Heat To make a fire hotter, tap the coals to remove their ash cover. To intensify the heat, push the coals together, and to lower the heat, spread the coals apart. Opening the vents on a covered grill raises the temperature, whereas partially closing them lowers the temperature.

DIRECT & INDIRECT GRILLING

Direct Method

This is the grilling method that is used most often: The food is placed directly over the heat source of a gas or charcoal grill. Similar to broiling, direct grilling sears the food, creating a wonderfully crisp, caramelized crust. The direct method cooks food fairly quickly, so it is best used for smaller foods such as kebabs, steaks, cut-up chicken, burgers, chops, and vegetables.

- For **gas grills**, preheat the grill to the desired temperature.

- For **charcoal grills**, pile the coals in the center of the grill and heat them to the desired temperature. Spread out the coals, and you're ready to grill.

- Place the grill rack 4 to 5 inches above the heat, and place the food on the rack directly over the hot coals.

Indirect Method

This grilling method is designed for larger pieces of meat that would char before they were cooked through if grilled using the direct method. In indirect grilling, the food is placed near—not over—the heat, which enables the food to cook slowly and evenly (like in oven roasting). The indirect method is ideal for cooking roasts, racks of ribs, briskets, whole chickens, whole turkeys, and other large cuts of meat.

- For **gas grills**, preheat one burner (for grills with three or more burners, preheat the two outer burners) to the desired temperature. Place the food on the grill rack over the unlit burner. Close the grill lid and grill as directed in the recipe (If the grill doesn't have a drip pan, place a disposable foil pan next to the lit burner and under the food.)

- For **charcoal grills**, mound the hot coals to one side of the grill, and prepare the fire to the desired temperature. Place a disposable foil drip pan next to the coals on the unheated portion of the grill to catch any drippings. Place the food on the grill rack over the unheated portion of the grill. Close the grill lid and grill as directed in the recipe.

FLAVORING THE FIRE

Rubs and marinades aren't the only ways to flavor food. The smoke from wood chips and herbs adds flavor too.

WOOD CHIPS AND CHUNKS Bags of small wood chips and larger wood chunks can be found in large hardware stores and in some specialty food stores.

• Soak the chips in enough water to cover for about 30 minutes, then drain. Sprinkle the chips directly over the hot briquettes. If using a gas grill, poke several holes in a disposable foil pan, spread the chips in the pan, and set it on top of a preheated burner.

• Soak large wood chunks in enough water to cover for 1 to 2 hours, then drain. Add the chunks to a charcoal grill along with the briquettes. Or when preheating a gas grill, poke holes in a disposable foil pan, put the chunks in the pan, and place it on top of a burner.

• Use oak and mesquite for beef and pork, and use hickory wood for turkey, chicken, and pork.

• Fruitwood, such as apple and cherry, are mild enough to use with chicken and seafood.

HERBS, SPICES, CITRUS, AND MORE There are other easy ways to flavor up the fire, including bay leaves, herb sprigs, citrus peel, and garlic cloves. Use the flavoring ingredient that complements the food being grilled.

• **Fresh Herb Sprigs** Soak several oregano, rosemary, or thyme sprigs in water for about 30 minutes, then place a few directly on the hot coals or a lit burner just before you put the food on the grill. As the sprigs burn up, add more to the fire. Use herb sprigs to flavor meat, poultry, and fish.

• **Citrus Zest** Soak long strips of lemon or orange zest in water about 30 minutes. Place a few directly on the hot coals or a lit burner just before you put the food on the grill. Add more to the fire as needed. Use citrus zest to flavor pork, poultry, fish, and vegetables.

• **Bay Leaves and Unpeeled Garlic Cloves** Soak bay leaves and garlic in water for about 30 minutes. Place directly on the hot coals or lit burner just before you put the food on the grill. Use bay leaves and garlic to flavor lamb, pork, poultry, fish, and vegetables.

GRILLING SAFETY

Keep these common-sense guidelines in mind so your backyard gatherings are as safe as they are delicious.

- Except for grills meant to be used indoors, always cook in the open air. You're safe under a carport or in the doorway of a garage, but never use a charcoal or gas grill indoors.

- Always spray the grill rack with nonstick spray *before* lighting the grill. Never spray the grill rack while the fire is alive—a dangerous flare-up could result.

- Never add liquid fire starter to an existing fire, as the stream of fluid could ignite.

- Keep an eye on the grill at all times, especially when children and pets are around.

- Don't wear loose or highly flammable clothing when grilling.

- If a minor flare up occurs, cover the grill until the flame subsides or squirt the fire with water.

- In case of a grease fire, cover a charcoal grill and close all vents. Turn off a gas grill at its source. If necessary, use a fire extinguisher.

- Clean out the ash pan of a charcoal grill only when the grill is completely cool—a hot ember could start a fire in the garbage can. Scrub the grill grid with a wire brush to get rid of food particles.

- Store propane cylinders and starter fluids outdoors, upright, and away from children. Keep out of sunlight or enclosed areas.

- Transfer cooked food from the grill to a clean plate to prevent cross contamination with the plate that contained the raw food.

- Always marinate meat, poultry, and fish in the refrigerator. Do not let them stand more than 30 minutes at room temperature before grilling.

- If you are using any leftover marinade from meat, poultry, or fish to serve with or brush on the grilled food, be sure to boil the marinade for at least 3 minutes to prevent the growth of bacteria. Otherwise, discard the leftover marinade.

TIME/TEMPERATURE CHART

(Note: Grilling times will vary depending on the grill. See manufacturer's booklet.)

BEEF

CUT	THICKNESS/WEIGHT	METHOD/HEAT	TIME
Steak	¾ inch	Direct Medium	8–10 min
Steak	1 inch	Direct Medium	10–12 min
Steak	1½ inches	Direct High; Indirect Medium	Sear 10 min; Grill 6–8 min
Flank Steak	1–1¼ pounds	Direct Medium-High	10–15 min
Tenderloin	3 pounds	Direct High; Indirect Medium	Sear 10 min; Grill 20–35 min
Hamburger	¾ inch thick	Direct Medium	8–12 min
Filet Mignon	3 ounces each	Direct Medium	8–10 min

PORK

CUT	THICKNESS/WEIGHT	METHOD/HEAT	TIME
Loin/Rib Chop	½–¾ inch	Direct Medium-High	10–15 min
Whole Tenderloin	1–1¼ pounds	Indirect Medium	25–30 min
Spareribs	2 pounds	Indirect Medium	1½–2 hours

LAMB

CUT	THICKNESS/WEIGHT	METHOD/HEAT	TIME
Loin/Rib Chop	¾ inch	Direct Medium-High	10–15 min
Butterflied Leg	2 pounds	Direct Medium	30 min

POULTRY

CUT	THICKNESS/WEIGHT	METHOD/HEAT	TIME
Boneless, Skinless Chicken Breasts	¼ pound each	Direct Medium	8–10 min
Bone-In Chicken Breast Halves	½ pound each	Direct Medium	25–35 min
Chicken Thighs	¼ pound each	Direct Medium-High	12–15 min
Whole Chicken	3–3½ pounds	Indirect Medium	1 hr–1 hr 20 min
Turkey Burger	¾ inch	Direct Medium	10–12 min
Game Hen	1–1½ pounds each	Direct Medium	30–40 min

FISH

CUT	THICKNESS/WEIGHT	METHOD/HEAT	TIME
Fish Fillet	¼–½ inch	Direct Medium-High	4–6 min
Fish Steak	½–1 inch	Direct Medium	6–10 min
Whole Fish	1–2 pounds	Indirect Medium	15–20 min
Shrimp	Medium–extra-large	Direct Medium	2–6 min

NIBBLES & STARTERS

Chapter 1

• • •

HUMMUS & SALAD–TOPPED PITAS

prep 15 MIN   *cook* 5 MIN   *serves* 8

4   (6-inch) whole-wheat pita
     breads, halved

1   (7-ounce) package baby
     spinach

½   English (seedless) cucumber,
     cut into ¼-inch dice

1   tomato, cut into ¼-inch dice

½   small red onion, thinly sliced

2   tablespoons orange juice

2   tablespoons lemon juice

2   teaspoons honey

1   teaspoon olive oil

1   teaspoon ground cumin

¼   teaspoon salt

¾   cup prepared hummus

1 Spray the grill rack with nonstick spray. Preheat the grill to medium-high or prepare a medium-high fire using the direct method (see page 13).

2 Lightly spray the pitas with nonstick spray. Place on the grill rack and grill, turning occasionally, until well marked, 3–4 minutes; set aside.

3 Combine the spinach, cucumber, tomato, and red onion in a large bowl. Whisk together the orange juice, lemon juice, honey, oil, cumin, and salt in a small bowl. Drizzle over the spinach mixture and toss to coat evenly.

4 Spread 1½ tablespoons hummus on each pita half. Top evenly with the spinach mixture.

PER SERVING (½ salad-topped pita): 149 Cal, 4 g Fat, 1 g Sat Fat, 0 g Trans Fat, 0 mg Chol, 325 mg Sod, 25 g Carb, 5 g Fib, 6 g Prot, 60 mg Calc. **POINTS** value: **3.**

HUMMUS &
SALAD–TOPPED PITAS

● ● ●

GRILLED TUNA & WHITE BEAN BRUSCHETTA

prep 20 MIN   *cook* 5 MIN   *serves* 8

1   (15½-ounce) can cannellini (white kidney) beans, rinsed and drained

1   tablespoon lemon juice

2   teaspoons extra-virgin olive oil

1   garlic clove, minced

½   teaspoon dried oregano

¾   teaspoon salt

1   (½-pound) tuna steak, about 1 inch thick

1   (8-ounce) baguette, cut on the diagonal into 16 slices

1½   tablespoons chopped fresh chives

2   small lemons, each cut into 4 wedges

1 Combine the beans, lemon juice, oil, garlic, oregano, and ¼ teaspoon of the salt in a medium bowl; coarsely mash with a fork. Set aside.

2 Spray the grill rack with nonstick spray. Preheat the grill to medium-high or prepare a medium-high fire using the direct method (see page 13).

3 Sprinkle the tuna with the remaining ½ teaspoon salt; lightly spray with nonstick spray. Place on the grill rack and grill 2–3 minutes on each side for medium-rare or until desired doneness. Transfer the tuna to a cutting board; let stand about 5 minutes.

4 Meanwhile, place the slices of bread on the grill rack and grill until well marked, 1–2 minutes on each side. With a long, thin knife, cut the tuna into 16 slices. Spread each slice of toast with about 1 tablespoon of the bean mixture; top with 1 slice of tuna and sprinkle evenly with the chives. Arrange the bruschetta and lemon wedges on a platter and serve at once.

PLAY IT SAFE
For optimum freshness, buy tuna from a fish store or supermarket with high turnover, especially if you like it medium-rare. Fresh tuna should look moist.

PER SERVING (2 bruschetta): 178 Cal, 5 g Fat, 1 g Sat Fat, 0 g Trans Fat, 17 mg Chol, 501 mg Sod, 24 g Carb, 5 g Fib, 12 g Prot, 63 mg Calc. **POINTS** value: **3.**

SMOKED CHICKEN & MUSHROOM QUESADILLAS

prep 20 MIN   *cook* 15 MIN   *serves* 16

1   (10-ounce) package white mushrooms, thinly sliced

¼   teaspoon salt

1   (1-pound) fully-cooked smoked boneless chicken breast, skin removed, thinly sliced crosswise

3   ounces reduced-fat soft (mild) goat cheese, crumbled

4   teaspoons seeded and chopped pickled jalapeño peppers

4   (8-inch) fat-free flour tortillas

½   cup prepared tomato salsa

1 Preheat the grill to medium-high or prepare a medium-high fire using the direct method (see page 13).

2 Spray a large grill-safe nonstick skillet with nonstick spray and place on the grill rack. Add the mushrooms and sprinkle with the salt; cook, stirring occasionally, until tender, about 8 minutes. Transfer the mushrooms to a small bowl.

3 Place one-fourth of the chicken, mushrooms, and goat cheese, and 1 teaspoon of the jalapeños on half of each tortilla. Fold the unfilled half of each tortilla over the filling, pressing down lightly.

4 Lightly spray the tortillas with nonstick spray. Place on the grill rack and grill until the quesadillas are lightly marked and the filling is heated through, about 3 minutes on each side. Cut each quesadilla into 4 wedges and serve with the salsa.

PER SERVING (1 quesadilla wedge and 1½ teaspoons salsa): 75 Cal, 2 g Fat, 1 g Sat Fat, 0 g Trans Fat, 16 mg Chol, 530 mg Sod, 7 g Carb, 1 g Fib, 8 g Prot, 32 mg Calc. **POINTS** value: **1.**

• • •

BEEF & BLUE CHEESE CROSTINI

prep 20 MIN   *cook* 15 MIN   *serves* 12

1   (1-pound) beef tenderloin, trimmed

½   teaspoon salt

¼   teaspoon black pepper

1   (20-inch) baguette

2   garlic cloves, peeled

2   tablespoons Dijon mustard

1   cup lightly packed tender watercress sprigs

¼   cup crumbled blue cheese

2   tablespoons chopped fresh chives

2   tablespoons finely chopped red onion

1 Spray the grill rack with nonstick spray. Preheat the grill to medium-high or prepare a medium-high fire using the direct method (see page 13).

2 Sprinkle the tenderloin with the salt and pepper. Place on the grill rack and grill, turning once, until an instant-read thermometer inserted into the center of the tenderloin registers 145°F for medium, about 12 minutes. Transfer to a cutting board and let stand 5 minutes. Slice the tenderloin across the grain into 24 thin slices.

3 Cut the baguette on the diagonal into 24 (½-inch) slices; lightly spray with nonstick spray. Place the slices on the grill rack and grill until well marked, about 2 minutes on each side. Rub one side of each baguette slice with the cut sides of the garlic. Spread each slice evenly with the mustard, then top with the watercress, beef, and blue cheese. Sprinkle evenly with the chives and red onion and arrange on a platter.

PER SERVING (2 crostini): 155 Cal, 6 g Fat, 2 g Sat Fat, 0 g Trans Fat, 19 mg Chol, 362 mg Sod, 14 g Carb, 2 g Fib, 12 g Prot, 44 mg Calc. **POINTS** value: **3.**

●●●

BEEF NEGIMAKI ✓

prep 10 MIN   *cook* 5 MIN   *serves* 8

1   pound beef tenderloin, trimmed and cut into 16 slices

6   tablespoons black bean sauce

2   teaspoons unseasoned rice vinegar

2   teaspoons minced peeled fresh ginger

16   (3½-inch) lengths of scallion

1 Spray the grill rack with olive oil nonstick spray. Prcheat the grill to medium-high or prepare a medium-high fire using the direct method (see page 13). If using wooden skewers, soak them in water 30 minutes.

2 Meanwhile, place the slices of beef in a single layer between 2 sheets of wax paper. With a meat mallet or rolling pin, lightly pound each slice to flatten slightly. Combine the bean sauce, vinegar, and ginger in a large bowl. Add the beef and toss to coat evenly.

3 Tightly wrap 1 slice of beef around each scallion length to make 16 rolls in all. Thread 2 beef rolls on each of 8 (6-inch) skewers.

4 Place the skewers on the grill rack and grill, turning occasionally, until the beef is cooked through, about 4 minutes. Serve hot or warm.

HOW WE DID IT

To make it easy to slice the beef uniformly, wrap it in plastic wrap and place in the freezer for about 30 minutes or until slightly frozen, so that it's very firm but not hard.

PER SERVING (2 negimaki): 108 Cal, 4 g Fat, 2 g Sat Fat, 0 g Trans Fat, 25 mg Chol, 127 mg Sod, 2 g Carb, 1 g Fib, 14 g Prot, 14 mg Calc. **POINTS** value: **2.**

GINGER CHICKEN
YAKITORI

●●●

GINGER CHICKEN YAKITORI

prep 10 MIN   *cook* 20 MIN   *serves* 6

3   tablespoons reduced-
    sodium soy sauce

2   tablespoons mirin

2   tablespoons sake or
    dry sherry

2   tablespoons grated peeled
    fresh ginger

2   teaspoons sugar

1   pound skinless boneless
    chicken thighs, cut into
    2-inch chunks

1   scallion, thinly sliced

1 Spray the grill rack with nonstick spray. Preheat the grill to medium-high or prepare a medium-high fire using the direct method (see page 13). If using wooden skewers, soak them in water 30 minutes.

2 Meanwhile, to make the sauce, combine the soy sauce, mirin, sake, ginger, and sugar in a small saucepan; bring to a boil over medium-high heat. Cook until the sauce is reduced to ⅓ cup, about 6 minutes. Remove the saucepan from the heat; set aside.

3 Thread the chicken on 6 (8-inch) skewers dividing it evenly. Place the skewers on the grill rack and grill, turning frequently and basting with the sauce, until the chicken is cooked through, about 10 minutes. Sprinkle the chicken with the sliced scallion. Serve hot or warm.

PER SERVING (1 chicken skewer): 145 Cal, 6 g Fat, 2 g Sat Fat, 0 g Trans Fat, 47 mg Chol, 398 mg Sod, 4 g Carb, 0 g Fib, 17 g Prot, 22 mg Calc. *POINTS* value: *3.*

GOOD IDEA

Grill a few extra whole scallions about 2 minutes on each side to serve with the chicken.

●●●

GRILLED SHRIMP COCKTAIL WITH CRANBERRY-GINGER HORSERADISH

prep 20 MIN   *cook* 5 MIN   *serves* 6

¾ cup canned whole-berry cranberry sauce

1 tablespoon prepared horseradish

2 teaspoons minced peeled fresh ginger

2 teaspoons grated lime zest

1 teaspoon lime juice

24 large shrimp (about 1 pound), peeled and deveined, tails left on if desired

½ teaspoon salt

¼ teaspoon black pepper

1 Spray the grill rack with nonstick spray. Preheat the grill to medium-high or prepare a medium-high fire using the direct method (see page 13). If using wooden skewers, soak them in water 30 minutes.

2 Combine the cranberry sauce, horseradish, ginger, and lime zest and juice in a small bowl until blended; set aside.

3 Thread 4 shrimp on each of 6 (8-inch) skewers and sprinkle with the salt and pepper.

4 Place the skewers on the grill rack and grill until the shrimp are just opaque in the center, 1–2 minutes on each side. Serve with the sauce.

PER SERVING (1 skewer and about 2 tablespoons sauce): 83 Cal, 0 g Fat, 0 g Sat Fat, 0 g Trans Fat, 47 mg Chol, 268 mg Sod, 14 g Carb, 1 g Fib, 5 g Prot, 14 mg Calc. **POINTS** value: **1.**

• • •

GRILLED CLAMS CASINO ☑

prep 15 MIN   *cook* 10 MIN   *serves* 8

2   teaspoons olive oil

2   slices Canadian bacon,
    finely chopped

1   small red bell pepper,
    finely diced

1   shallot, minced

1   garlic clove, minced

¼   teaspoon salt

1   tablespoon chopped
    fresh parsley

1   teaspoon grated lemon zest

2   dozen littleneck clams,
    shucked, bottom shells
    reserved

1 Preheat the grill to medium-high or prepare a medium high fire using the direct method (see page 13).

2 Heat the oil in a small nonstick skillet over medium heat. Add the bacon, bell pepper, shallot, garlic, and salt; cook, stirring, until softened, 6–8 minutes. Remove the skillet from the heat; stir in the parsley and lemon zest.

3 Place 1 clam in each shell and top each with about 1 teaspoon of the bell pepper mixture. Place the clams on the grill rack and grill, covered, until just cooked through, about 3 minutes. Serve at once.

PER SERVING (3 clams): 71 Cal, 2 g Fat, 0 g Sat Fat, 0 g Trans Fat, 23 mg Chol, 189 mg Sod, 3 g Carb, 0 g Fib, 9 g Prot, 32 mg Calc. **POINTS** value: **2.**

PLAY IT SAFE

When purchasing clams (or mussels), make sure the shells are tightly closed, and avoid chipped or broken shells.

●●●

GREEK-STYLE EGGPLANT ROLLS ☑

prep 20 MIN   *cook* 6 MIN   *serves* 4

¼ cup crumbled fat-free feta cheese

1 tomato, diced

2 scallions, finely chopped

2 tablespoons chopped fresh mint

½ teaspoon dried oregano

½ teaspoon salt

1 (1-pound) eggplant, cut lengthwise into 8 slices

1 tablespoon lemon juice

2 teaspoons extra-virgin olive oil

Lemon wedges (optional)

1 Combine the feta, tomato, scallions, 1 tablespoon of the mint, the oregano, and ¼ teaspoon of the salt in a medium bowl; set aside.

2 Spray the grill rack with olive oil nonstick spray. Preheat the grill to medium-high or prepare a medium-high fire using the direct method (see page 13).

3 Lightly spray the eggplant slices with nonstick spray. Place on the grill rack and grill until well marked and tender, about 3 minutes on each side. Transfer to a plate; let cool slightly.

4 To assemble the rolls, spoon about 2 tablespoons of the tomato mixture on the wider end of each slice of eggplant. Roll up tightly and place, seam side down, on a platter. Whisk together the lemon juice, oil, and the remaining 1 tablespoon mint and ¼ teaspoon salt in a small bowl; drizzle over the rolls. Garnish with the lemon wedges if using.

PER SERVING (2 eggplant rolls): 87 Cal, 3 g Fat, 1 g Sat Fat, 0 g Trans Fat, 1 mg Chol, 411 mg Sod, 13 g Carb, 3 g Fib, 4 g Prot, 91 mg Calc. **POINTS** value: **1.**

• • •

GRILLED ARTICHOKE HEARTS WITH TOMATO VINAIGRETTE ☑

prep 20 MIN   *cook* 30 MIN   *serves* 8

2   lemons, halved

4   large artichokes (about 10 ounces each)

6   plum tomatoes, cut into ¼-inch dice

3   tablespoons chopped fresh basil

1   shallot, minced (about 2 tablespoons)

1   tablespoon balsamic vinegar

2   teaspoons extra-virgin olive oil

½   teaspoon salt

½   teaspoon black pepper

1 Bring a nonreactive large pot of water to a boil. Meanwhile, squeeze the lemons into a bowl of cold water; drop in the lemon halves. Bend back and snap off the dark green leaves from an artichoke until you reach the pale green leaves. With a knife, peel the stem, leaving 1 inch attached. Slice 1 inch off the top of the artichoke; drop into the lemon water. Repeat.

2 Place the artichokes and lemon halves in the boiling water and return the water to a boil. Reduce the heat and simmer, covered, until a small knife inserted into the bottom of an artichoke goes in easily, about 20 minutes. With tongs, transfer the artichokes to a colander and hold under cold running water to stop the cooking; drain well. Cut each artichoke lengthwise in half. With a small spoon, scoop out and discard the fuzzy choke and any violet-colored leaves surrounding the choke; set aside.

3 Preheat the grill to medium-high or prepare a medium-high fire using the direct method (see page 13).

4 To make the vinaigrette, combine the tomatoes, basil, shallot, vinegar, oil, ¼ teaspoon of the salt, and ¼ teaspoon of the pepper in a small bowl; set aside. Spray the artichokes with olive oil nonstick spray and sprinkle with the remaining ¼ teaspoon salt and ¼ teaspoon pepper. Place, cut side down, on the grill rack and grill, turning occasionally, until very tender and well marked, about 10 minutes. Transfer the artichokes to a platter and spoon the vinaigrette on top. Serve at once.

PER SERVING (1 artichoke half and ½ cup vinaigrette): 64 Cal, 2 g Fat, 0 g Sat Fat, 0 g Trans Fat, 0 mg Chol, 222 mg Sod, 11 g Carb, 5 g Fib, 3 g Prot, 42 mg Calc. ***POINTS*** value: **1.**

• • •

GRILLED PEAR SALAD WITH WALNUTS & GOAT CHEESE

prep 20 MIN   *cook* 5 MIN   *serves* 4

2   Bosc pears, quartered and cored

1   tablespoon tarragon vinegar

1   tablespoon orange juice

1   tablespoon honey

2   teaspoons extra-virgin olive oil

1   teaspoon Dijon mustard

¼   teaspoon salt

5   cups lightly packed torn frisée lettuce

4   tablespoons crumbled reduced-fat soft (mild) goat cheese

4   tablespoons walnuts, toasted and chopped

1 Spray the grill rack with nonstick spray. Preheat the grill to medium-high or prepare a medium-high fire using the direct method (see page 13).

2 Lightly spray the pears with nonstick spray. Place, cut side down, on the grill rack and grill until tender and well marked, about 2 minutes on each side. Transfer the pears to a plate; set aside.

3 To make the dressing, whisk together the vinegar, orange juice, honey, oil, mustard, and salt in a medium bowl. Put the frisée in a large bowl and drizzle with the dressing; toss to coat evenly. Divide the lettuce evenly among 4 plates and top each with 2 pear wedges. Sprinkle each salad with 1 tablespoon of the goat cheese and 1 tablespoon of the walnuts.

PER SERVING (1 salad): 145 Cal, 7 g Fat, 2 g Sat Fat, 0 g Trans Fat, 4 mg Chol, 228 mg Sod, 20 g Carb, 4 g Fib, 3 g Prot, 61 mg Calc. **POINTS** value: **3.**

FOOD NOTE

Frisée is a member of the chicory family. It has feathery pale green leaves and a pleasantly bitter taste. Choose frisée that is firm and without any browning.

GRILLED PEAR SALAD
WITH WALNUTS & GOAT CHEESE

• • •

ASPARAGUS WITH PROSCIUTTO & PARMESAN

prep 5 MIN   *cook* 5 MIN   *serves* 4

1   bunch (1 pound) asparagus, trimmed

1   teaspoon extra-virgin olive oil

¼   teaspoon salt

¼   teaspoon black pepper

1   ounce prosciutto, finely chopped (about 2 tablespoons)

1   tablespoon grated Parmesan cheese

1 Spray the grill rack with nonstick spray. Preheat the grill to medium-high or prepare a medium-high fire using the direct method (see page 13).

2 Toss together the asparagus, oil, salt, and pepper until coated evenly. Place the asparagus on the grill rack and grill, turning often, until tender and well marked, about 4 minutes. Transfer the asparagus to a platter. Scatter the prosciutto on top and sprinkle with the Parmesan.

PER SERVING (¼ of asparagus): 43 Cal, 3 g Fat, 1 g Sat Fat, 0 g Trans Fat, 5 mg Chol, 232 mg Sod, 3 g Carb, 1 g Fib, 3 g Prot, 36 mg Calc. **POINTS** value: **1.**

• • •

GRILLED ANTIPASTO SALAD ☑

prep 20 MIN   *cook* 10 MIN   *serves* 4

2   (4-inch) portobello mushrooms, stems removed, caps halved

2   Cubanelle peppers, halved lengthwise

1   red bell pepper, quartered lengthwise

1   small eggplant (about ¾ pound), quartered lengthwise

2   large tomatoes, cut crosswise in half

¾   teaspoon salt

½   teaspoon black pepper

10   pitted brine-cured kalamata olives

1   tablespoon capers, drained

2   tablespoons chopped fresh basil

2   tablespoons balsamic vinegar

¾   teaspoon dried oregano

1 Spray the grill rack with olive oil nonstick spray. Preheat the grill to medium-high or prepare a medium-high fire using the direct method (see page 13).

2 Combine the mushrooms, Cubanelle and bell peppers, eggplant, and tomatoes in a large bowl. Lightly spray with nonstick spray and sprinkle with the salt and black pepper; toss to coat evenly.

3 Place the vegetables on the grill rack and grill, turning occasionally, until tender and well marked, about 8 minutes for the mushrooms, peppers, and eggplant and about 4 minutes for the tomatoes.

4 Arrange the vegetables on a platter and sprinkle with the olives. Combine the capers, basil, vinegar, and oregano in a small bowl and sprinkle over the vegetables. Serve warm or at room temperature.

PER SERVING (¼ of antipasto): 95 Cal, 2 g Fat, 0 g Sat Fat, 0 g Trans Fat, 0 mg Chol, 595 mg Sod, 19 g Carb, 6 g Fib, 4 g Prot, 38 mg Calc. **POINTS** value: **1.**

TRY IT

Cubanelles (koo-ba-NELLS) are large elongated sweet peppers that range in color from yellow to pale green. They are also known as Italian frying peppers.

ROASTED CORN
& CHIVE SOUP

• • •

ROASTED CORN & CHIVE SOUP

prep 20 MIN   *cook* 50 MIN   *serves* 6

4	ears of corn
2	teaspoons olive oil
1	onion, chopped
2	garlic cloves, minced
¼	teaspoon salt
¼	teaspoon black pepper
2	(14½-ounce) cans reduced-sodium chicken broth
1	(½-pound) Yukon Gold potato, peeled and cut into 1-inch chunks
¼	cup fat-free half-and-half
2	tablespoons chopped fresh chives

1 Gently pull back the husks from the corn and remove the silk. Place the husks back over the corn. Place in a large bowl and add enough water to cover. Let stand about 20 minutes; drain.

2 Meanwhile, spray the grill rack with nonstick spray. Preheat the grill to medium or prepare a medium fire using the direct method (see page 13).

3 Place the corn on the grill rack and grill, turning, until the husks are lightly charred, 20–25 minutes. When cool enough to handle, remove the husks; discard. Stand an ear of corn in a large bowl. Using a long serrated knife, cut the kernels from the cob. Repeat with the remaining corn. (You should have about 2 cups corn.) Reserve the cobs. Set aside ⅓ cup of the corn.

4 Heat the oil in a nonstick Dutch oven over medium heat. Add the onion, garlic, salt, and pepper. Cook, stirring, until tender, about 8 minutes. Add enough water to the broth to equal 4 cups. Add the corn, the reserved cobs, broth, and potato to the Dutch oven; bring to a boil over medium-high heat. Reduce the heat and simmer, covered, until the potato is tender, about 15 minutes. Remove and discard the cobs. Remove the Dutch oven from the heat; let the soup cool about 5 minutes.

5 Puree the soup, in batches, in a blender. Return the soup to the Dutch oven and stir in the half-and-half; reheat over medium heat. Ladle into 6 bowls and sprinkle evenly with the chives and reserved corn.

PER SERVING (1 cup): 154 Cal, 3 g Fat, 0 g Sat Fat, 0 g Trans Fat, 1 mg Chol, 444 mg Sod, 30 g Carb, 4 g Fib, 5 g Prot, 33 mg Calc. **POINTS** value: **3.**

●●●

CHILLED BEET SOUP WITH CUCUMBER & SCALLION ☑

prep 20 MIN   *cook* 1 HR   *serves* 6

4 large beets (about 2½ pounds), trimmed

1 red onion, halved through the root end

3 fresh thyme sprigs

2 (14½-ounce) cans reduced-sodium chicken broth

2 cups water

1 tablespoon lemon juice

6 tablespoons fat-free sour cream

1 small cucumber, peeled, seeded, and cut into ¼-inch dice

2 scallions, thinly sliced

1 Preheat the grill to medium or prepare a medium fire using the direct method (see page 13).

2 Spray an 18 x 20-inch sheet of heavy-duty foil with olive oil nonstick spray. Place the beets, red onion, and thyme sprigs in the middle of the foil; lightly spray with nonstick spray. Bring the 2 opposite long sides of the foil up to meet in the center; fold the edges over twice to make a tight seal. Double fold the open sides to seal the packet.

3 Place the packet on the grill rack and grill until the beets are fork-tender, about 1 hour. Wearing oven mitts, transfer the packet to a cutting board. Open the packet, being careful to avoid the steam that is released; discard the thyme sprigs.

4 When the beets are cool enough to handle, slip off the peel and coarsely chop. Add enough water to the broth to equal 4 cups. Puree the beets and onion with the broth, in batches, in a food processor or blender. Transfer to a large bowl and stir in the water and lemon juice. Cover and refrigerate until well chilled, at least 4 hours or up to overnight. Ladle the soup into 6 bowls and top evenly with the sour cream, cucumber, and scallions.

HOW WE DID IT

As much as we love beets, we do not love getting our hands stained from beets! To prevent magenta hands, slip on a pair of disposable latex gloves.

PER SERVING (1½ cups soup, 1 tablespoon sour cream, about 3 tablespoons cucumber, and 2 teaspoons scallion): 109 Cal, 2 g Fat, 0 g Sat Fat, 0 g Trans Fat, 1 mg Chol, 172 mg Sod, 19 g Carb, 4 g Fib, 6 g Prot, 59 mg Calc. **POINTS** value: **2.**

● ● ●

TOMATO-CHIPOTLE SALSA & CHIPS

prep 20 MIN   *cook* NONE   *serves* 6

1   pound plum tomatoes, halved lengthwise and seeded

½   small red onion, finely chopped

1   tablespoon finely chopped fresh cilantro

½   chipotle en adobo, minced

1   small garlic clove, minced

1½   teaspoons olive oil

1½   teaspoons lime juice

⅛   teaspoon salt

48   unsalted baked tortilla chips

1 Preheat the grill to medium-high or prepare a medium-high fire using the direct method (see page 13).

2 Spray the tomatoes with nonstick spray. Place, cut side down, on the grill rack and grill until lightly charred, about 4 minutes on each side.

3 Chop the tomatoes and put in a serving bowl. Stir in all the remaining ingredients except the tortilla chips. Serve at once or cover and set aside at room temperature up to 2 hours. Serve with the tortilla chips. Makes 1½ cups salsa.

PER SERVING (¼ cup salsa and 8 chips): 104 Cal, 2 g Fat, 0 g Sat Fat, 0 g Trans Fat, 0 mg Chol, 82 mg Sod, 20 g Carb, 2 g Fib, 2 g Prot, 11 mg Calc. ***POINTS*** value: **2.**

NO-FUSS MAIN DISHES

Chapter 2

• • •

BALSAMIC-GLAZED FLANK STEAK WITH ARUGULA

prep 10 MIN *cook* 20 MIN *serves* 4

¾ cup balsamic vinegar

1 tablespoon packed brown sugar

1 garlic clove, minced

1 teaspoon olive oil

½ teaspoon salt

¼ teaspoon black pepper

1 (1-pound) flank steak, trimmed

6 cups lightly packed baby arugula

1 Spray the grill rack with nonstick spray. Preheat the grill to medium-high or prepare a medium-high fire using the direct method (see page 13).

2 Meanwhile, combine the vinegar and brown sugar in a small saucepan; bring to a boil over medium-high heat. Boil until the mixture is reduced to a syrupy glaze, about 8 minutes. Remove the saucepan from the heat; set aside.

3 Combine the garlic, oil, salt, and pepper in a small bowl; rub the mixture on both sides of the steak. Place on the grill rack and grill until an instant-read thermometer inserted into the side of the steak registers 145°F for medium, about 5 minutes on each side. Transfer to a cutting board and let stand 5 minutes. Cut the steak across the grain into 12 slices.

4 Divide the arugula evenly among 4 plates and top each portion with 3 slices of steak. Drizzle with the reserved balsamic glaze and serve at once.

PER SERVING (1½ cups arugula, 3 slices steak, and 1 tablespoon glaze): 222 Cal, 9 g Fat, 3 g Sat Fat, 0 g Trans Fat, 49 mg Chol, 341 mg Sod, 5 g Carb, 1 g Fib, 27 g Prot, 62 mg Calc. **POINTS** value: **5.**

PASTRAMI-STYLE FLANK STEAK

prep 10 MIN   *cook* 10 MIN   *serves* 4

1 tablespoon black peppercorns

1 tablespoon fennel seeds

1 tablespoon coriander seeds

1 tablespoon packed brown sugar

2 garlic cloves

¼ teaspoon salt

1 (1-pound) flank steak, trimmed

1 Combine all the ingredients except the flank steak in a spice grinder or mini–food processor; pulse until coarsely ground. Press the spice mixture on both sides of the steak. Place the steak in a large zip-close plastic bag. Squeeze out the air and seal the bag. Refrigerate, turning the bag occasionally, at least 1 hour or up to 8 hours.

2 Meanwhile, spray the grill rack with nonstick spray. Preheat the grill to medium-high or prepare a medium-high fire using the direct method (see page 13).

3 Place the steak on the grill rack and grill until an instant-read thermometer inserted into the side of the steak registers 145°F for medium, about 5 minutes on each side. Transfer the steak to a cutting board and let stand about 5 minutes. Cut the steak across the grain into 12 slices.

MAKE IT CORE

To fit this recipe into the **Core Plan,** omit the brown sugar.

PER SERVING (3 slices steak): 208 Cal, 8 g Fat, 3 g Sat Fat, 0 g Trans Fat, 49 mg Chol, 186 mg Sod, 6 g Carb, 2 g Fib, 27 g Prot, 45 mg Calc. **POINTS** value: **4.**

• • •

BISTECCA ALLA PIZZAIOLA WITH GARLIC BREAD

prep 10 MIN   *cook* 20 MIN   *serves* 4

1   tablespoon olive oil

3   garlic cloves, 2 minced and 1 halved

2   cups canned peeled Italian tomatoes with juice

¾   teaspoon salt

¼   teaspoon crushed red pepper

¼   cup chopped fresh basil

1   (1-pound) boneless sirloin steak, trimmed

½   (8-ounce) baguette

1   teaspoon dried oregano

1 Spray the grill rack with nonstick spray. Preheat the grill to medium-high or prepare a medium-high fire using the direct method (see page 13).

2 Meanwhile, to make the sauce, heat the oil in a medium saucepan over medium-high heat. Add the minced garlic and cook, stirring constantly, until softened, about 1 minute. Add the tomatoes, ½ teaspoon of the salt, and the crushed red pepper; bring to a boil. Reduce the heat and simmer, stirring occasionally with a wooden spoon and breaking up the tomatoes, until the sauce thickens slightly, 7–10 minutes. Remove the saucepan from the heat and stir in the basil; keep warm.

3 Sprinkle the steak with the remaining ¼ teaspoon salt. Place on the grill rack and grill until an instant-read thermometer inserted into the center of the steak registers 145°F for medium, about 5 minutes on each side. Transfer the steak to a cutting board and let stand about 5 minutes.

4 Cut the bread lengthwise in half, then crosswise into 4 equal pieces. Spray the cut sides of the bread with olive oil nonstick spray and sprinkle with the oregano. Place the bread, cut side down, on the grill rack and grill until nicely browned, 2–4 minutes. Rub the cut sides of the bread with the cut sides of the remaining garlic clove.

5 Cut the steak into 12 slices and serve with the sauce and garlic bread.

PER SERVING (3 slices steak, generous ⅓ cup sauce, and 1 piece bread): 356 Cal, 10 g Fat, 2 g Sat Fat, 0 g Trans Fat, 64 mg Chol, 960 mg Sod, 34 g Carb, 3 g Fib, 32 g Prot, 97 mg Calc. **POINTS** value: **7.**

BISTECCA ALLA PIZZAIOLA
WITH GARLIC BREAD

BOURBON-BARBECUED BEEF WITH CREOLE SLAW

prep **15 MIN**   *cook* **20 MIN**   *serves* **4**

¼   cup fat-free mayonnaise

1   tablespoon Creole or spicy brown mustard

1   tablespoon apple-cider vinegar

1   teaspoon sugar

1   (16-ounce) bag coleslaw mix

1   teaspoon canola oil

½   pound shiitake mushrooms, stems removed and caps sliced

1   onion, finely chopped

1   cup prepared barbecue sauce

3   tablespoons bourbon

1   tablespoon chopped fresh parsley

2   (8-ounce) boneless strip steaks, trimmed

¼   teaspoon salt

1 To make the coleslaw, combine the mayonnaise, mustard, vinegar, and sugar in a large bowl. Add the coleslaw mix, tossing well to combine. Cover and refrigerate up to 4 hours.

2 Spray the grill rack with nonstick spray. Preheat the grill to medium-high or prepare a medium-high fire using the direct method (see page 13).

3 Meanwhile, to make the barbecue sauce, heat the oil in a large nonstick skillet over medium-high heat. Add the mushrooms and onion; cook, stirring, until softened, about 8 minutes. Stir together the barbecue sauce and bourbon in a small bowl. Stir into the mushroom mixture and bring to a boil. Reduce the heat and simmer, stirring occasionally, until the sauce thickens slightly, 3–5 minutes. Remove the skillet from the heat and stir in the parsley. Cover and keep warm.

4 Sprinkle the steaks with the salt. Place on the grill rack and grill until an instant-read thermometer inserted into the center of a steak registers 145°F for medium, about 5 minutes on each side. Transfer the steaks to a cutting board and let stand about 5 minutes. Cut each steak in half and serve with the barbecue sauce and coleslaw.

TRY IT

A little bourbon or dark rum added to prepared barbecue sauce is an easy way to add flavor. If you prefer a little more heat, add some hot sauce.

PER SERVING (½ steak, about ⅓ cup sauce, and generous ¾ cup coleslaw): 361 Cal, 9 g Fat, 3 g Sat Fat, 0 g Trans Fat, 44 mg Chol, 1030 mg Sod, 41 g Carb, 5 g Fib, 27 g Prot, 104 mg Calc. **POINTS** value: **7.**

●●●

PERFECT BURGERS WITH ALL THE FIXINGS

prep 10 MIN   *cook* 10 MIN   *serves* 4

1 pound ground lean beef
   (7% fat or less)

3 tablespoons minced onion

1 tablespoon Worcestershire
   sauce

½ teaspoon salt

¼ teaspoon black pepper

4 multigrain hamburger buns,
   split

4 green leaf lettuce leaves

4 thin slices red onion

4 tablespoons ketchup

1 Spray the grill rack with nonstick spray. Preheat the grill to medium-high or prepare a medium-high fire using the direct method (see page 13).

2 Meanwhile, combine the beef, minced onion, Worcestershire sauce, salt, and pepper in a medium bowl. With damp hands, shape the mixture into 4 (½-inch-thick) patties.

3 Place the patties on the grill rack and grill until an instant-read thermometer inserted into the side of a burger registers 160°F for well done, about 5 minutes on each side.

4 Place the burgers on the bottoms of the buns and top each one with 1 lettuce leaf, 1 slice red onion, and 1 tablespoon ketchup.

PER SERVING (1 garnished burger): 292 Cal, 9 g Fat, 3 g Sat Fat, 0 g Trans Fat, 64 mg Chol, 700 mg Sod, 27 g Carb, 2 g Fib, 26 g Prot, 67 mg Calc. **POINTS** value: **6.**

VIETNAMESE BEEF AND
NOODLE SALAD

VIETNAMESE BEEF & NOODLE SALAD

prep 20 MIN　　　*cook* 15 MIN　　　*serves* 6

4　ounces rice stick noodles

3　tablespoons lime juice

3　tablespoons packed
　　brown sugar

2　tablespoons reduced-
　　sodium soy sauce

2　teaspoons grated peeled
　　fresh ginger

1　teaspoon Asian fish sauce

½　teaspoon Thai red
　　curry paste

¾　pound round steak, cut on
　　the diagonal into ¼-inch strips

1　(4-ounce bag) watercress,
　　coarsely chopped

1　cup bean sprouts

1　tomato, chopped

½　cup matchstick-cut carrots

¼　cup coarsely chopped
　　fresh mint

¼　cup coarsely chopped
　　fresh cilantro

2　tablespoons dry-roasted
　　peanuts, chopped

1 Preheat the grill to medium-high or prepare a medium-high fire using the direct method (see page 13).

2 Meanwhile, place the noodles in a large bowl and add enough hot water to cover. Let the noodles stand until softened, about 10 minutes. Drain in a colander, then rinse under running cold water; drain again. Transfer the noodles to a large bowl.

3 To make the dressing, whisk together the lime juice, brown sugar, soy sauce, ginger, fish sauce, and curry paste in a small bowl. Put the beef in a medium bowl. Add 2 tablespoons of the dressing and toss to coat well. Reserve the remaining dressing.

4 Spray a grill wok or vegetable grill topper with nonstick spray and place on the grill rack. Add the beef and stir-fry just until brown, 2–3 minutes. Transfer the beef to a plate.

5 Add all the remaining ingredients except the peanuts to the noodles in the bowl; toss well to combine. Mound the noodle mixture on a large platter and top with the beef. Drizzle with the reserved dressing and sprinkle with the peanuts.

PER SERVING (about 1 cup): 218 Cal, 4 g Fat, 1 g Sat Fat, 0 g Trans Fat, 32 mg Chol, 330 mg Sod, 28 g Carb, 2 g Fib, 17 g Prot, 54 mg Calc. **POINTS** value: **4.**

●●●

JERK PORK WITH CURRIED PINEAPPLE SALSA

prep 20 MIN   *cook* 30 MIN   *serves* 4

1   tablespoon jerk seasoning

1   (1-pound) pork tenderloin, trimmed

1½ teaspoons curry powder

½   pineapple, peeled, cut into ½-inch slices, and cored

½   small papaya, peeled, seeded, and cut into ¼-inch pieces

2   tablespoons chopped fresh cilantro

1½ teaspoons grated lime zest

1½ tablespoons lime juice

1½ teaspoons minced peeled fresh ginger

1½ teaspoons honey

1 Spray the grill rack with nonstick spray. Preheat the grill to medium-high or prepare a medium-high fire using the direct method (see page 13).

2 Rub the jerk seasoning all over the pork and lightly spray with nonstick spray. Place on the grill rack and grill, turning, until an instant-read thermometer inserted into the center of the pork registers 160°F for medium, 20–25 minutes. Transfer the pork to cutting board and let stand about 5 minutes.

3 Meanwhile, sprinkle the curry powder on both sides of the pineapple slices. Place on the grill rack and grill until tender and well marked, about 4 minutes on each side. Transfer the pineapple to a cutting board and let cool.

4 To make the salsa, cut the cooled pineapple into ¼-inch pieces and transfer to a serving bowl. Add the remaining ingredients and toss to combine. Cut the pork into 12 slices and serve with the salsa.

HOW WE DID IT

To core sliced pineapple quickly, cut out the hard center with a 1-inch round cookie cutter.

PER SERVING (3 slices pork and generous ½ cup salsa): 194 Cal, 5 g Fat, 1 g Sat Fat, 0 g Trans Fat, 67 mg Chol, 58 mg Sod, 14 g Carb, 2 g Fib, 25 g Prot, 39 mg Calc. **POINTS** value: **4.**

SALTIMBOCCA ROLLS WITH GRILLED ARTICHOKES

prep 20 MIN   *cook* 10 MIN   *serves* 4

1 (1-pound) pork tenderloin, trimmed and cut on the diagonal into 8 slices

1 tablespoon chopped fresh sage

4 (½-ounce) slices lean ham, halved

4 (½-ounce) slices reduced-fat Swiss cheese, halved

2 (14-ounce) cans artichoke hearts, drained and halved

1 teaspoon olive oil

¼ teaspoon salt

¼ teaspoon black pepper

1 Spray the grill rack with nonstick spray. Preheat the grill to medium-high or prepare a medium-high fire using the direct method (see page 13). If using wooden skewers, soak them in water 30 minutes.

2 Meanwhile, place the slices of pork in a single layer between 2 sheets of wax paper. With a meat mallet or rolling pin, lightly pound to ¼-inch thickness. Sprinkle the cutlets with the sage, then top each one with 1 slice of ham and 1 slice of Swiss cheese. Roll up the cutlets beginning with a short side, then thread each roll on 2 (10-inch) parallel skewers, holding the skewers about ¾ inch apart.

3 Place the pork rolls on the grill rack and grill, turning occasionally, until an instant-read thermometer inserted into the center of a roll registers 160°F for medium, 10–12 minutes. Transfer to a platter; keep warm.

4 Combine the remaining ingredients in a medium bowl and toss well to combine. Place a vegetable grill topper on the grill rack. Place the artichokes on the topper in a single layer and grill, turning occasionally, until lightly browned and tender, about 6 minutes. Serve with the pork.

PER SERVING (2 pork rolls and ¾ cup artichokes): 271 Cal, 7 g Fat, 2 g Sat Fat, 0 g Trans Fat, 80 mg Chol, 839 mg Sod, 17 g Carb, 8 g Fib, 36 g Prot, 211 mg Calc. **POINTS** value: **5.**

• • •

HERBED PORK CHOPS WITH WARM MUSHROOM SALAD

prep 10 MIN   *cook* 15 MIN   *serves* 4

1   teaspoon dried sage

¾   teaspoon salt

½   teaspoon dried thyme

½   teaspoon black pepper

4   (6-ounce) bone-in pork loin chops, ½ inch thick, trimmed

½   pound cremini mushrooms, halved

¼   pound shiitake mushrooms, stems removed and caps sliced

¼   pound oyster mushrooms

2   teaspoons olive oil

¼   cup lightly packed flat-leaf parsley leaves

1   garlic clove, minced

2   tablespoons Parmesan cheese shavings

1½   cups hot cooked whole-wheat couscous

1 Spray the grill rack with nonstick spray. Preheat the grill to medium-high or prepare a medium-high fire using the direct method (see page 13).

2 Meanwhile, combine the sage, ½ teaspoon of the salt, the thyme, and ¼ teaspoon of the pepper in a small bowl. Sprinkle the sage mixture on both sides of the pork chops.

3 Place the chops on the grill rack and grill, turning, until an instant-read thermometer inserted into the side of a chop registers 160°F for medium, 4–6 minutes on each side. Transfer the chops to a platter; keep warm.

4 Combine the cremini, shiitake, and oyster mushrooms, the oil, and the remaining ¼ teaspoon salt and ¼ teaspoon pepper in a large bowl. Spray a vegetable grill topper with nonstick spray and place on the grill rack. Spread the mushroom mixture on the topper and grill, stirring occasionally, until the mushrooms are tender, 6–8 minutes. Return the mushrooms to the bowl; stir in the parsley and garlic. Add the mushroom mixture to the platter and sprinkle with the Parmesan shavings. Serve with the couscous.

PER SERVING (1 pork chop, ½ cup mushroom salad, and generous ⅓ cup couscous): 323 Cal, 13 g Fat, 4 g Sat Fat, 0 g Trans Fat, 73 mg Chol, 551 mg Sod, 21 g Carb, 4 g Fib, 33 g Prot, 75 mg Calc. **POINTS** value: **7.**

HERBED PORK CHOPS WITH WARM MUSHROOM SALAD

• • •

ORANGE & ROSEMARY–RUBBED PORK CHOPS WITH NECTARINES

prep 10 MIN   *cook* 15 MIN   *serves* 4

1	tablespoon grated orange zest
2	teaspoons fennel seeds, crushed
2	teaspoons chopped fresh rosemary
1	teaspoon olive oil
½	teaspoon salt
¼	teaspoon black pepper
4	(6-ounce) bone-in pork loin chops, ¾ inch thick, trimmed
4	nectarines (4 ounces each), halved and pitted

1 Spray the grill rack with olive oil nonstick spray. Preheat the grill to medium-high or prepare a medium-high fire using the direct method (see page 13).

2 Meanwhile, to make the herb rub, mix together the orange zest, fennel seeds, rosemary, oil, salt, and pepper in a small bowl until the mixture forms a paste. Rub the paste on both sides of the pork chops.

3 Place the chops on the grill rack and grill until an instant-read thermometer inserted into the side of a chop registers 160°F for medium, 5–6 minutes on each side. Transfer the chops to a plate; keep warm.

4 Meanwhile, lightly spray the cut sides of the nectarines with nonstick spray. Place, cut side down, on the grill rack and grill, turning, until tender and well marked, about 4 minutes on each side. Serve with the pork.

HOW WE DID IT

A simple way to crush fennel seeds is to gather them into a pile on a cutting board and lightly spray them with nonstick spray. With a large knife, chop the seeds.

PER SERVING (1 pork chop and 2 nectarine halves): 243 Cal, 10 g Fat, 3 g Sat Fat, 0 g Trans Fat, 71 mg Chol, 338 mg Sod, 12 g Carb, 2 g Fib, 26 g Prot, 27 mg Calc. **POINTS** value: **5.**

GRILLED RACK OF LAMB WITH MINTED CRUMBS

prep 20 MIN   *cook* 20 MIN   *serves* 4

1   8-rib rack of lamb
     (1½ pounds), frenched

¼   teaspoon salt

¼   teaspoon black pepper

1   tablespoon plain dried
     bread crumbs

1   tablespoon chopped
     fresh mint

2   teaspoons finely chopped
     fresh parsley

2   teaspoons grated
     lemon zest

1   teaspoon olive oil

1   garlic clove, minced

1 Spray the grill rack with nonstick spray. Preheat the grill to medium-high or prepare a medium-high fire using the direct method (see page 13).

2 Sprinkle the lamb all over with the salt and pepper. Place on the grill rack and grill, turning, until nicely browned, about 10 minutes. Transfer the lamb to a plate; set aside. (Leave the grill on.)

3 Combine the remaining ingredients in a small bowl. Press the crumb mixture evenly on the meaty side of the lamb, then lightly spray the crumb mixture with nonstick spray. Return the lamb, crumbed side up, to the grill rack and grill until an instant-read thermometer inserted into the center of the rack (not touching bone) registers 145°F for medium, about 10 minutes. (Do not turn the lamb.) Transfer to a cutting board and cover loosely with foil. Let stand about 10 minutes, then slice between every other bone to make 4 double chops.

PER SERVING (1 double chop): 140 Cal, 8 g Fat, 3 g Sat Fat, 0 g Trans Fat, 44 mg Chol, 201 mg Sod, 2 g Carb, 0 g Fib, 13 g Prot, 19 mg Calc. **POINTS** value: **3.**

LEMONGRASS PORK
PATTIES WITH ASIAN
CARROT-APPLE SALAD

● ● ●

LEMONGRASS PORK PATTIES WITH ASIAN CARROT-APPLE SALAD

prep 20 MIN   *cook* 10 MIN   *serves* 4

PATTIES

1   pound ground lean pork

2   tablespoons reduced-sodium soy sauce

1   tablespoon finely chopped lemongrass

1   shallot, minced

1   teaspoon Asian (dark) sesame oil

1   garlic clove, minced

DRESSING AND SALAD

2   tablespoons unseasoned rice vinegar

1   tablespoon minced peeled fresh ginger

1   teaspoon packed brown sugar

1   teaspoon reduced-sodium soy sauce

1   (10-ounce) bag matchstick-cut carrots

1   Granny Smith apple, peeled, cored, and cut into ½-inch pieces

3   tablespoons chopped fresh mint or small mint leaves

1 Spray the grill rack with nonstick spray. Preheat the grill to medium-high or prepare a medium-high fire using the direct method (see page 13).

2 Meanwhile, to make the patties, combine all the patty ingredients in a medium bowl. With damp hands, shape the mixture into 4 (½-inch-thick) patties.

3 Place the patties on the grill rack and grill, turning occasionally, until an instant-read thermometer inserted into the side of a patty registers 160°F for medium, 8–10 minutes. Transfer to a platter and keep warm.

4 To make the dressing and salad, whisk together the vinegar, ginger, brown sugar, and soy sauce in a serving bowl. Add the remaining ingredients and toss to coat well. Serve with the patties.

PER SERVING (1 patty with 1¼ cups salad): 229 Cal, 6 g Fat, 2 g Sat Fat, 0 g Trans Fat, 72 mg Chol, 413 mg Sod, 16 g Carb, 3 g Fib, 27 g Prot, 42 mg Calc. **POINTS** value: **4.**

●●●

CALABRIAN-STYLE LAMB CHOPS ☑

prep 30 MIN   *cook* 30 MIN   *serves* 4

1 red bell pepper, halved

1 yellow bell pepper, halved

1 teaspoon olive oil

1 small red onion, finely chopped

1 garlic clove, minced

½ cup canned peeled Italian tomatoes with juice

8 brine-cured green olives, pitted and chopped

½ teaspoon salt

1 tablespoon chopped fresh parsley

4 (¼-pound) bone-in lamb rib chops, about ¾ inch thick, trimmed

2 cups hot cooked brown rice

1 Spray the grill rack with olive oil nonstick spray. Preheat the grill to medium-high or prepare a medium-high fire using the direct method (see page 13).

2 Place the bell peppers on the grill rack and grill, turning occasionally, until tender, about 10 minutes. Transfer the peppers to a cutting board. When cool enough to handle, cut into 1-inch pieces; set aside. (Leave the grill on.)

3 Heat the oil in a large nonstick skillet over medium-high heat. Add the red onion and garlic; cook, stirring often, until tender, 3–4 minutes. Add the bell peppers, tomatoes, olives, and ¼ teaspoon of the salt. Bring to a boil over medium-high heat. Reduce the heat and simmer, covered, until the flavors are blended, about 10 minutes. Remove the skillet from the heat. Stir in the parsley; keep warm.

4 Sprinkle the lamb chops with the remaining ¼ teaspoon salt. Place on the grill rack and grill, turning occasionally, until an instant-read thermometer inserted into the side of a chop registers 145°F for medium, about 10 minutes. Transfer the lamb chops to a platter and spoon the bell pepper sauce alongside. Serve with the rice.

EXPRESS LANE

To make the sauce in less time, instead of grilling your own peppers, use brine-packed roasted red and yellow peppers from a jar. Just drain, chop, and add to the sauce.

PER SERVING (1 lamb chop, about ⅓ cup sauce, and ½ cup rice): 339 Cal, 14 g Fat, 4 g Sat Fat, 0 g Trans Fat, 69 mg Chol, 779 mg Sod, 30 g Carb, 5 g Fib, 24 g Prot, 51 mg Calc. **POINTS** value: **7.**

● ● ●

CHICKEN BREASTS STUFFED WITH HERBED GOAT CHEESE

prep 15 MIN   *cook* 15 MIN   *serves* 4

3   tablespoons chopped fresh basil

1   tablespoon chopped fresh parsley

1   tablespoon chopped fresh dill

2   teaspoons chopped fresh tarragon

2   teaspoons grated lemon zest

½   cup crumbled reduced-fat soft (mild) goat cheese

4   (¼-pound) skinless boneless chicken breast halves

½   teaspoon salt

¼   teaspoon black pepper

1 Spray the grill rack with nonstick spray. Preheat the grill to medium-high or prepare a medium-high fire using the direct method (see page 13).

2 Meanwhile, combine the basil, parsley, dill, tarragon, and lemon zest in a small bowl. Transfer 1 tablespoon of the herb mixture to a cup; set aside. Add the goat cheese to the remaining mixture; mix well with a fork.

3 Make a pocket in a chicken breast half by inserting a sharp small knife into the thickest part of the breast and gently moving the knife back and forth until a small pocket is formed. Repeat with the remaining chicken breasts, then enlarge the pockets with your fingers. Fill each pocket evenly with the herb mixture then secure each opening with a toothpick. Lightly spray the chicken with nonstick spray. Sprinkle with the salt, pepper, and reserved herb mixture.

4 Place the chicken on the grill rack and grill until well marked and cooked through, 8–10 minutes on each side.

PER SERVING (1 stuffed chicken breast): 188 Cal, 7 g Fat, 4 g Sat Fat, 0 g Trans Fat, 76 mg Chol, 422 mg Sod, 1 g Carb, 0 g Fib, 28 g Prot, 45 mg Calc. **POINTS** value: **4.**

TURKISH KEBABS WITH
SAFFRON RICE AND
MARINATED GRILL-ROASTED
PEPPERS, PAGE 151

TURKISH KEBABS WITH SAFFRON RICE

prep 10 MIN   *cook* 50 MIN   *serves* 4

KEBABS

1   tablespoon tomato paste

1   teaspoon paprika

½   teaspoon salt

½   teaspoon cinnamon

½   teaspoon ground cumin

¼   teaspoon ground allspice

1   pound boneless lean lamb,
    trimmed and cut into
    1-inch chunks

RICE

1   teaspoon olive oil

1   onion, finely chopped

1   cup brown basmati rice

2¼ cups reduced-sodium
    chicken broth

¼   teaspoon saffron threads,
    lightly crushed

¼   teaspoon salt

1 To make the kebabs, mix together all of the kebab ingredients except the lamb in a large bowl; add the lamb and toss until evenly coated. Transfer the lamb to a large zip-close plastic bag. Squeeze out the air and seal the bag. Refrigerate, turning the bag occasionally, at least 1 hour or up to overnight.

2 To make the rice, heat the oil in a medium saucepan over medium-high heat. Add the onion and cook, stirring frequently, until softened, 3–5 minutes. Add the rice and cook, stirring constantly, until lightly toasted, 2–3 minutes. Add the broth, saffron, and salt; bring to a boil. Reduce the heat and simmer, covered, until the rice is tender, 40–45 minutes. Remove the saucepan from the heat. Let stand 10 minutes, then fluff the rice with a fork; keep warm.

3 Meanwhile, spray the grill rack with olive oil nonstick spray. Preheat the grill to medium-high or prepare a medium-high fire using the direct method (see page 13). If using wooden skewers, soak them in water 30 minutes.

4 Thread the lamb on 4 (8-inch) skewers dividing it evenly. Place the skewers on the grill rack and grill the lamb, turning occasionally, until medium doneness, 6–8 minutes. Serve with the rice.

PER SERVING (1 skewer and ¾ cup rice): 377 Cal, 10 g Fat, 3 g Sat Fat, 0 g Trans Fat, 75 mg Chol, 854 mg Sod, 40 g Carb, 6 g Fib, 30 g Prot, 48 mg Calc. ***POINTS*** value: **8.**

• • •

BEST-EVER LEMON-ROASTED CHICKEN

prep **15 MIN**   *cook* **1 HR 20 MIN**   *serves* **6**

2   cups applewood, mesquite, or hickory chips

1   tablespoon chopped fresh rosemary

1   tablespoon chopped fresh tarragon

2   teaspoons grated lemon zest

1   garlic clove, minced

1   teaspoon olive oil

½   teaspoon salt

1   (3½-pound) chicken, without giblets

1   lemon, cut into 4 wedges

2   garlic cloves, peeled

2   fresh rosemary sprigs

1 Remove the grill rack and preheat the grill to medium or prepare a medium fire using the indirect method (see page 13). Soak the wood chips in a bowl of water about 30 minutes.

2 Meanwhile, combine the chopped rosemary, tarragon, lemon zest, garlic, oil, and salt in a small bowl. With your fingers, loosen the skin on the chicken breasts, legs, and thighs. Rub the herb mixture on the meat under the skin; press the skin back into place. Put the lemon wedges, garlic cloves, and rosemary sprigs in the cavity of the chicken. Tuck the wings under the chicken and tie the legs together tightly with kitchen string.

3 Drain the wood chips. If using a gas grill, place the chips in a small disposable foil pan with a few holes poked in and place on a lit burner. If using a charcoal grill, sprinkle the chips over the coals. Spray the grill rack with olive oil nonstick spray then place on the grill.

4 Place the chicken, breast side up, on the cooler portion of the grill rack. Grill, covered, without turning, until an instant read thermometer inserted into a thigh registers 180°F, about 1 hour 20 minutes. Transfer the chicken to a carving board and let stand about 10 minutes before carving. Discard the ingredients in the cavity of the chicken. Remove the skin before eating.

GOOD IDEA

Grill assorted vegetables, such as red onion wedges, whole bell peppers, and sliced zucchini to serve alongside.

PER SERVING (⅙ of chicken): 182 Cal, 8 g Fat, 2 g Sat Fat, 0 g Trans Fat, 81 mg Chol, 275 mg Sod, 0 g Carb, 0 g Fib, 27 g Prot, 18 mg Calc. **POINTS** value: **4.**

BEST-EVER
LEMON-ROASTED
CHICKEN

MOJITO-BARBECUED
CHICKEN AND MEXICAN
GRILLED CORN, PAGE 142

MOJITO-BARBECUED CHICKEN

prep **15 MIN**   *cook* **20 MIN**   *serves* **6**

2   tablespoons grated lime zest (about 2 limes)

¼   cup lime juice

¼   cup orange juice

2   tablespoons chopped fresh mint

1   tablespoon honey

2   garlic cloves, minced

2   teaspoons olive oil

1   teaspoon ground cumin

½   teaspoon salt

1   (3½–pound) chicken, cut into 6 pieces, skin removed from all but wings

1   lime, cut into wedges

Fresh mint sprigs

1 To make the marinade, combine the lime zest and juice, orange juice, mint, honey, garlic, oil, cumin, and salt in a small bowl. Transfer half of the lime mixture to a covered container and refrigerate. Transfer the remaining lime mixture to a large zip-close plastic bag and add the chicken. Squeeze out the air and seal the bag; turn to coat the chicken. Refrigerate, turning the bag occasionally, at least 2 hours or up to overnight. Remove the chicken from the marinade; scrape off and discard the excess marinade.

2 Spray the grill rack with nonstick spray. Preheat the grill to medium or prepare a medium fire using the direct method (see page 13).

3 Place the chicken on the grill rack and grill, turning occasionally, until cooked through, 20–30 minutes.

4 Pour the reserved lime mixture into a small saucepan and bring to a simmer.

5 Transfer the chicken to a platter and spoon the warm lime sauce on top. Garnish with the lime wedges and mint sprigs. Remove the skin from the wings before eating.

PER SERVING (⅙ of chicken): 212 Cal, 8 g Fat, 2 g Sat Fat, 0 g Trans Fat, 81 mg Chol, 279 mg Sod, 7 g Carb, 1 g Fib, 27 g Prot, 29 mg Calc. **POINTS** value: **5.**

• • •

CORNMEAL-CRUSTED CHICKEN WITH CORN-TOMATO RAGOUT ☑

prep 20 MIN   *cook* 20 MIN   *serves* 4

4   ears of corn, husks and silk removed

1   red bell pepper, cut into ¼-inch dice

1   tomato, cut into ¼-inch dice

½   small vidalia onion, finely chopped (about ⅓ cup)

1   jalapeño pepper, seeded and minced (wear gloves to prevent irritation)

2   tablespoons apple-cider vinegar

1   tablespoon chopped fresh parsley

2   teaspoons extra-virgin olive oil

¾   teaspoon salt

⅛   teaspoon black pepper

¼   cup cornmeal, preferably stone ground

1   teaspoon Cajun seasoning

4   (¼-pound) skinless boneless chicken cutlets

1 Spray the grill rack with olive oil nonstick spray. Preheat the grill to medium-high or prepare a medium-high fire using the direct method (see page 13).

2 To make the ragout, place the corn on the grill rack and grill, turning, until well marked, about 8 minutes. Transfer the corn to a cutting board and let cool about 5 minutes. With a long serrated knife, cut the kernels off the cobs and transfer to a serving bowl. Add the bell pepper, tomato, onion, jalapeño pepper, vinegar, parsley, oil, ¼ teaspoon of the salt, and the black pepper; mix well.

3 Spray a large grill-safe nonstick skillet with nonstick spray and place on the grill rack to preheat. Mix together the cornmeal, Cajun seasoning, and remaining ½ teaspoon salt on a sheet of wax paper. Coat the chicken cutlets with the cornmeal mixture, pressing lightly so it adheres. Lightly spray the chicken on both sides with nonstick spray.

4 Add the chicken to the skillet and cook, turning, until lightly browned and cooked through, about 8 minutes. Serve with the ragout.

PER SERVING (1 chicken cutlet and 1 cup ragout): 325 Cal, 8 g Fat, 2 g Sat Fat, 0 g Trans Fat, 68 mg Chol, 660 mg Sod, 36 g Carb, 6 g Fib, 30 g Prot, 26 mg Calc. **POINTS** value: **6.**

CHICKEN SATAY WITH RED CURRY–PEANUT SAUCE

prep 20 MIN   *cook* 15 MIN   *serves* 4

¼   cup light (reduced-fat) coconut milk

¼   cup reduced-fat peanut butter

2   tablespoons reduced-sodium soy sauce

1   tablespoon grated peeled fresh ginger

1   tablespoon packed brown sugar

½   teaspoon Thai red curry paste

1   tablespoon chopped fresh cilantro

4   (¼-pound) skinless boneless chicken breast halves, cut into 1½-inch chunks

1   red bell pepper, cut into 2-inch pieces

1   yellow bell pepper, cut into 2-inch pieces

4   scallions, cut into 3-inch lengths

½   teaspoon salt

1 Spray the grill rack with nonstick spray. Preheat the grill to medium-high or prepare a medium-high fire using the direct method (see page 13). If using wooden skewers, soak them in water 30 minutes.

2 Meanwhile, to make the dipping sauce, combine the coconut milk, peanut butter, soy sauce, ginger, brown sugar, and curry paste in a small saucepan and set over medium heat. Cook, stirring constantly, until the mixture is smooth and heated through, about 3 minutes. Remove the saucepan from the heat and stir in the cilantro. Transfer to a serving bowl; set aside.

3 Thread the chicken, bell peppers, and scallions alternately on 4 (10-inch) skewers. Sprinkle with the salt, then spray with nonstick spray. Place the skewers on the grill rack and grill, turning occasionally, until the chicken is cooked through and the vegetables are tender, 10–12 minutes. Serve with the peanut sauce.

PER SERVING (1 skewer and 3 tablespoons sauce): 284 Cal, 11 g Fat, 3 g Sat Fat, 0 g Trans Fat, 68 mg Chol, 729 mg Sod, 17 g Carb, 2 g Fib, 31 g Prot, 41 mg Calc. **POINTS** value: **6.**

**MOROCCAN-STYLE CHICKEN
WITH OLIVES**

●●●

MOROCCAN-STYLE CHICKEN WITH OLIVES

prep 10 MIN   *cook* 15 MIN   *serves* 4

2   teaspoons grated lemon zest

1   teaspoon olive oil

1   teaspoon grated peeled
     fresh ginger

1   teaspoon fennel seeds,
     crushed

¾   teaspoon cinnamon

¾   teaspoon ground cumin

¾   teaspoon ground cardamom

½   teaspoon salt

4   (¼-pound) skinless boneless
     chicken thighs

2   lemons or limes, each cut into
     4 wedges

8   pitted brine-cured kalamata
     olives, sliced

1   tablespoon chopped
     flat-leaf parsley

1 Combine the lemon zest, oil, ginger, fennel seeds, cinnamon, cumin, cardamom, and salt in a large zip-close plastic bag and add the chicken. Squeeze out the air and seal the bag; turn to coat the chicken. Refrigerate, turning the bag occasionally, at least 1 hour or up to 4 hours.

2 Meanwhile, spray the grill rack with olive oil nonstick spray. Preheat the grill to medium-high or prepare a medium-high fire using the direct method (see page 13).

3 Place the chicken on the grill rack and grill, turning occasionally, until cooked through, 12–15 minutes. Just before the chicken is done, place the lemon wedges on the grill rack and grill until lightly marked and slightly softened, 2–3 minutes. Transfer the chicken and lemon to a platter. Scatter the olives on top of the chicken and sprinkle with the parsley.

PER SERVING (1 chicken thigh and 2 olives): 219 Cal, 11 g Fat, 3 g Sat Fat, 0 g Trans Fat, 71 mg Chol, 283 mg Sod, 5 g Carb, 2 g Fib, 25 g Prot, 59 mg Calc. ***POINTS*** value: **5.**

GOOD IDEA

Grilling the chicken over mesquite chips adds another tempting layer of flavor. See page 14 for directions.

●●●

CORNISH HENS UNDER A BRICK ☑

prep **15 MIN**   *cook* **40 MIN**   *serves* **4**

1   tablespoon chopped
    fresh parsley

1   tablespoon chopped
    fresh rosemary

1   garlic clove, minced

2   teaspoons olive oil

½   teaspoon crushed red pepper

½   teaspoon salt

2   (1½-pound) Cornish game hens

1 Spray the grill rack with olive oil nonstick spray. Preheat the grill to medium-high or prepare a medium-high fire using the indirect method (see page 13). Separately wrap 2 clean bricks or the outside of a large cast-iron skillet in heavy-duty foil.

2 Meanwhile, combine all the ingredients except the hens in a small bowl; set aside.

3 With kitchen shears, cut along each side of the backbone of one hen; discard the backbone. Turn the hen, breast side up and open flat, then use the palm of your hand to flatten the breast slightly. With your fingers, carefully loosen the skin on the breasts, legs, and thighs. Rub half of the herb mixture on the meat under the skin, then press the skin back in place; tuck the wings under the hen. Repeat with the second hen.

4 Place the hens, skin side down, on the cooler portion of the grill rack. Place a brick (or cast-iron skillet) on top of each hen and close the grill. Grill 20 minutes. Wearing heavy grill-safe oven mitts or using sturdy tongs, set the bricks aside. Turn the hens and grill until an instant-read thermometer inserted into a thigh registers 180°F, about 20 minutes longer. Transfer the hens to a cutting board and let stand about 10 minutes. With scissors, cut each hen in half by cutting along the breastbone. Remove the skin before eating.

PER SERVING (½ Cornish hen): 224 Cal, 8 g Fat, 2 g Sat Fat, 0 g Trans Fat, 159 mg Chol, 391 mg Sod, 1 g Carb, 0 g Fib, 35 g Prot, 24 mg Calc. **POINTS** value: **5.**

● ● ●

TURKEY TOSTADAS WITH SMOKY TOMATILLO SALSA

prep 10 MIN   *cook* 15 MIN   *serves* 4

6	tomatillos (about ¾ pound), papery husks removed, rinsed
¼	cup chopped fresh cilantro
2	tablespoons lime juice
2	teaspoons honey
1	chipotle en adobo
1	garlic clove
½	teaspoon salt
4	(¼-pound) turkey cutlets
4	(6-inch) corn tortillas
1	cup mixed baby salad greens

1 Spray the grill rack with nonstick spray. Preheat the grill to medium-high or prepare a medium-high fire using the direct method (see page 13).

2 To make the salsa, place the tomatillos on the grill rack and grill, turning often, until softened and lightly charred, 6–8 minutes. Transfer to a food processor or blender; add the cilantro, lime juice, honey, chipotle en adobo, garlic, and ¼ teaspoon of the salt; pulse until smooth. Transfer the salsa to a small bowl; set aside.

3 Sprinkle the turkey cutlets with the remaining ¼ teaspoon salt and lightly spray with nonstick spray. Place on the grill rack and grill until well marked and cooked through, about 4 minutes on each side. Transfer the cutlets to a cutting board. Let cool about 5 minutes, then thinly slice.

4 Place the tortillas in a single layer on the grill rack and warm through, about 30 seconds on each side. Place 1 tortilla on each of 4 plates. Top each with ¼ cup salad greens, 1 sliced turkey cutlet, and 2 tablespoons salsa.

PER SERVING (1 tostada): 208 Cal, 2 g Fat, 1 g Sat Fat, 0 g Trans Fat, 75 mg Chol, 748 mg Sod, 18 g Carb, 3 g Fib, 29 g Prot, 47 mg Calc. **POINTS** value: **4.**

• • •

GRILLED KIELBASA WITH CARAWAY CABBAGE

prep 15 MIN   *cook* 15 MIN   *serves* 4

2   teaspoons light butter

1   (16-ounce) bag coleslaw mix

1   teaspoon caraway seeds

¼   teaspoon salt

1   (1-pound) low-fat turkey
     kielbasa, cut into 12 chunks

2   apples, cored and cut into
     1-inch chunks

2   red onions, cut into 1½ inch
     wedges

¼   cup apple jelly, melted

1   teaspoon chopped
     fresh thyme

1 Spray the grill rack with nonstick spray. Preheat the grill to medium-high or prepare a medium-high fire using the direct method (see page 13). If using wooden skewers, soak in water 30 minutes.

2 Place a large grill-safe nonstick skillet on the grill rack. Add the butter and heat until it melts. Add the coleslaw, caraway seeds, and salt; cook, stirring frequently, just until the coleslaw begins to wilt, about 5 minutes. Remove from the heat and keep warm.

3 Thread the kielbasa, apples, and red onions alternately on each of 4 (10-inch) skewers, Combine the jelly and thyme in a small bowl; brush over the skewers.

4 Place the skewers on the grill rack and grill, turning occasionally, until the sausage, apples, and onions are well marked and tender, 6–8 minutes. Serve with the cabbage.

ZAP IT

The jelly can be melted in a microwave. Combine the jelly and thyme in a cup and microwave on High until bubbly, 8–10 seconds.

PER SERVING (1 skewer and ½ cup cabbage): 310 Cal, 6 g Fat, 3 g Sat Fat, 0 g Trans Fat, 52 mg Chol, 1152 mg Sod, 35 g Carb, 6 g Fib, 16 g Prot, 117 mg Calc. ***POINTS*** value: **6.**

GRILLED SALMON NIÇOISE ☑

prep **30 MIN**   *cook* **30 MIN**   *serves* **4**

1   pound small red potatoes, scrubbed and halved

½   pound green beans, trimmed

½   pound asparagus, trimmed

4   (6-ounce) salmon fillets

½   teaspoon salt

¼   teaspoon black pepper

2   tablespoons reduced-sodium chicken broth

2   tablespoons white-wine vinegar

1   tablespoon chopped fresh basil

1   teaspoon chopped fresh tarragon

2   teaspoons extra-virgin olive oil

1   teaspoon Dijon mustard

4   Boston lettuce leaves

½   cup cherry tomatoes, halved

8   pitted brine-cured niçoise olives

1   tablespoon capers, rinsed and drained

1 Combine the potatoes with enough cold water to cover in a large saucepan; bring to a boil over medium-high heat. Reduce the heat and simmer until tender, 15–20 minutes. With a slotted spoon, transfer the potatoes to a plate. Return the water to a boil. Add the green beans and cook 2 minutes. Add the asparagus to the water and cook until the beans and asparagus are tender, about 2 minutes longer. Drain in a colander, then rinse under cold running water to stop the cooking.

2 Meanwhile, spray the grill rack with olive oil nonstick spray. Preheat the grill to medium-high or prepare a medium-high fire using the direct method (see page 13).

3 Sprinkle the salmon with ¼ teaspoon of the salt and the pepper; lightly spray with nonstick spray. Place on the grill rack and grill, turning once, until just opaque in the center, about 8 minutes. Transfer to a cutting board. Let cool about 5 minutes, then cut into 1-inch chunks.

4 Spray the cut sides of the potatoes with nonstick spray. Place, cut side down, on the grill rack and grill, turning once, until well marked, 2–3 minutes. Transfer to a plate; set aside.

5 To make the dressing, whisk together the broth, vinegar, basil, tarragon, oil, mustard, and the remaining ¼ teaspoon salt in a small bowl. Line a platter with the lettuce and arrange the potatoes, green beans and asparagus, salmon, and cherry tomatoes in piles on the lettuce. Drizzle with the dressing and sprinkle with the olives and capers. Remove the salmon skin before eating.

PER SERVING (about 2 cups): 392 Cal, 14 g Fat, 3 g Sat Fat, 0 g Trans Fat, 111 mg Chol, 582 mg Sod, 27 g Carb, 6 g Fib, 40 g Prot, 86 mg Calc. **POINTS** value: **8.**

• • •

SALMON TOPPED WITH GINGER-SCALLION PESTO ☑

prep 10 MIN   *cook* 10 MIN   *serves* 4

3   tablespoons finely chopped parsley

3   tablespoons finely chopped cilantro

3   tablespoons finely chopped scallion

1   tablespoon minced peeled fresh ginger

1   garlic clove, minced

3   tablespoons water

1   tablespoon lemon juice

2   teaspoons extra-virgin olive oil

½   teaspoon salt

4   (6-ounce) salmon steaks

1 Spray the grill rack with olive oil nonstick spray. Preheat the grill to medium-high or prepare a medium-high fire using the direct method (see page 13).

2 Meanwhile, to make the pesto, stir together the parsley, cilantro, scallion, ginger, garlic, water, lemon juice, oil, and ¼ teaspoon of the salt in a serving dish. Set aside.

3 Sprinkle the salmon with the remaining ¼ teaspoon salt. Place on the grill rack and grill until well marked and just opaque in the center, about 4 minutes on each side. Serve with the pesto. Remove the salmon skin before eating.

PER SERVING (1 salmon steak and 2 tablespoons pesto): 234 Cal, 11 g Fat, 3 g Sat Fat, 0 g Trans Fat, 95 mg Chol, 385 mg Sod, 2 g Carb, 0 g Fib, 31 g Prot, 28 mg Calc. **POINTS** value: **6.**

• • •

RED SNAPPER WITH CHUNKY ORANGE-AVOCADO RELISH ☑

prep 25 MIN   *cook* 20 MIN   *serves* 4

1   tablespoon chopped fresh oregano

2   teaspoons olive oil

½   teaspoon salt

1   (3-pound) cleaned whole red snapper

½   lemon, cut into 4 slices

4   fresh oregano sprigs

2   navel oranges, peeled and cut into sections

3   scallions, thinly sliced

¼   cup chopped fresh cilantro

3   large pitted brine-cured green olives, coarsely chopped

1   tablespoon grated lime zest

1   tablespoon lime juice

1   small avocado, peeled, pitted, and cut into ½-inch pieces

1 Spray the grill rack with olive oil nonstick spray. Preheat the grill to medium-high or prepare a medium-high fire using the direct method (see page 13).

2 Combine the oregano, oil, and salt in a cup. Score the fish skin, making 3 (½-inch-deep) diagonal cuts, about 1½ inches apart, on each side of the fish. Rub the oregano mixture over the fish. Place the lemon slices and oregano sprigs inside the cavity of the fish.

3 Place the fish on the grill rack and grill 10 minutes. With 2 spatulas, gently roll the fish over and grill until just opaque in the center, about 8 minutes longer.

4 Meanwhile, to make the relish, combine the orange sections, scallions, cilantro, olives, and lime zest and juice in a medium bowl; gently stir in the avocado. Transfer the fish to a platter. Discard the lemon slices and oregano sprigs. Serve with the relish. Remove the fish skin before eating.

PER SERVING (¼ of fish and ½ cup relish): 279 Cal, 11 g Fat, 2 g Sat Fat, 0 g Trans Fat, 90 mg Chol, 485 mg Sod, 13 g Carb, 5 g Fib, 34 g Prot, 75 mg Calc. **POINTS** value: **6.**

● ● ●

TUNA WITH MANGO-STRAWBERRY SALAD

prep 15 MIN   *cook* 10 MIN   *serves* 4

1   shallot, minced

1   tablespoon apple-cider
    vinegar

1   tablespoon lime juice

2   teaspoons honey

1   teaspoon extra-virgin
    olive oil

½   teaspoon salt

4   (5-ounce) tuna steaks,
    ¾ inch thick

4   cups mixed baby salad
    greens

1   mango, peeled, pitted, and
    cubed (about 1 cup)

1   cup strawberries, hulled and
    quartered

1 Spray the grill rack with nonstick spray. Preheat the grill to medium-high or prepare a medium-high fire using the direct method (see page 13).

2 Meanwhile, to make the dressing, whisk together the shallot, vinegar, lime juice, honey, oil, and ¼ teaspoon of the salt in a small bowl; set aside.

3 Sprinkle the tuna with the remaining ¼ teaspoon salt. Place on the grill rack and grill until well marked but still pink in the center, about 2 minutes on each side for medium-rare doneness.

4 Transfer the tuna to a cutting board and let stand about 5 minutes, then cut into ¼-inch slices. Divide the salad greens, mango, and strawberries among 4 plates. Top evenly with the tuna and drizzle with the dressing.

PER SERVING (1 plate): 262 Cal, 9 g Fat, 2 g Sat Fat, 0 g Trans Fat, 84 mg Chol, 390 mg Sod, 17 g Carb, 3 g Fib, 29 g Prot, 55 mg Calc. **POINTS** value: **5.**

TUNA WITH MANGO-STRAWBERRY SALAD

•••

COD WITH SALSA CRUDA ☑

prep 10 MIN   *cook* 10 MIN   *serves* 4

1   cup grape tomatoes, halved

1   cup yellow pear tomatoes, halved

¼   cup minced red onion

8   small pitted brine-cured green olives, chopped

1   tablespoon chopped fresh parsley

1   tablespoon grated lemon zest

1   tablespoon lemon juice

1   teaspoon extra-virgin olive oil

1   teaspoon capers, drained

1   garlic clove, minced

¼   teaspoon crushed red pepper

4   (6-ounce) cod fillets

¾   teaspoon Mexican or taco seasoning

1 Spray the grill rack with olive oil nonstick spray. Preheat the grill to medium-high or prepare a medium-high fire using the direct method (see page 13).

2 Meanwhile, to make the salsa, combine the tomatoes, red onion, olives, parsley, lemon zest and juice, oil, capers, garlic, and crushed red pepper in a medium bowl; set aside.

3 Sprinkle the cod with the Mexican seasoning and lightly spray with nonstick spray.

4 Place the cod on the grill rack and grill until just opaque in the center, about 3 minutes on each side. Serve with the salsa.

PER SERVING (1 cod fillet and ½ cup salsa): 201 Cal, 4 g Fat, 1 g Sat Fat, 0 g Trans Fat, 90 mg Chol, 284 mg Sod, 6 g Carb, 2 g Fib, 33 g Prot, 46 mg Calc. **POINTS** value: **4.**

● ● ●

ASIAN-STYLE HALIBUT WITH PEA SHOOT SALAD

prep 20 MIN   *cook* 10 MIN   *serves* 4

5   tablespoons mirin or
     dry sherry

3   tablespoons red miso

1   tablespoon honey

1   teaspoon Asian (dark)
     sesame oil

4   (6-ounce) halibut fillets,
     about 1¼ inches thick

2   tablespoons red-wine
     vinegar

1   teaspoon reduced-sodium
     soy sauce

1   teaspoon grated peeled
     fresh ginger

1   (4-ounce) bag pea shoots

8   radishes with tops, trimmed
     and halved lengthwise

1   carrot, thinly sliced

¼   cup lightly packed fresh
     mint leaves

1 Combine 3 tablespoons of the mirin, the miso, honey, and sesame oil in a large zip-close plastic bag; add the halibut fillets. Squeeze out the air and seal the bag; turn to coat the fish. Refrigerate, turning the bag occasionally, at least 30 minutes or up to 1 hour.

2 Meanwhile, spray the grill rack with nonstick spray. Preheat the grill to medium-high or prepare a medium-high fire using the direct method (see page 13).

3 Remove the fish from the marinade; discard the marinade. Place the fish on the grill rack and grill until just opaque in the center, about 5 minutes on each side. Transfer the fish to a plate; keep warm.

4 To make the salad, whisk together the remaining 2 tablespoons mirin, the vinegar, soy sauce, and ginger in a small bowl. Combine the pea shoots, radishes, carrot, and mint in a serving bowl. Drizzle with the dressing and toss to coat evenly. Serve with the halibut.

PER SERVING (1 halibut fillet and 1½ cups salad): 200 Cal, 3 g Fat, 1 g Sat Fat, 0 g Trans Fat, 90 mg Chol, 334 mg Sod, 7 g Carb, 1 g Fib, 34 g Prot, 84 mg Calc. **POINTS** value: **4.**

TRY IT

Pea shoots are the tender vines of young green peas. These sweet pea–flavored leaves are available in farmers' markets and specialty food stores.

• • •

SPICY LINGUINE WITH GRILLED SHRIMP & CLAMS ☑

prep 20 MIN   *cook* 25 MIN   *serves* 6

½   pound whole-wheat linguine

1   tablespoon olive oil

3   garlic cloves, minced

¼   teaspoon crushed red pepper

3   plum tomatoes, chopped

½   cup reduced-sodium chicken broth

1   tablespoon lemon juice

¾   teaspoon salt

¼   cup coarsely chopped flat-leaf parsley

2   teaspoons grated lemon zest

1   dozen littleneck clams, scrubbed

½   pound large shrimp, shelled and deveined

½   teaspoon black pepper

1 Cook the linguine according to the package directions omitting the salt if desired. Drain and keep warm.

2 Meanwhile, preheat the grill to medium-high or prepare a medium-high fire using the direct method (see page 13).

3 Add the oil to a large grill-safe nonstick skillet and place on the grill rack. Add the garlic and crushed red pepper; cook, stirring constantly, until fragrant, about 1 minute. Add the tomatoes and cook, stirring, until softened, about 3 minutes. Add the broth, lemon juice, and ½ teaspoon of the salt; bring to a boil. Remove the skillet from the heat. Stir in the parsley and lemon zest; keep warm.

4 Place the clams on the grill rack and grill, covered, until the shells open, 3–4 minutes. Discard any clams that do not open. Add the clams with their liquid to the sauce in the skillet; keep warm.

5 Meanwhile, thread the shrimp on 2 (12-inch) metal skewers. Sprinkle with the remaining ¼ teaspoon salt and the pepper and spray with olive oil nonstick spray. Place the skewers on the grill rack and grill the shrimp until lightly browned and just opaque in the center, 1–2 minutes on each side. Slide the shrimp off the skewers and add to the sauce in the skillet. Transfer the linguine to a serving bowl and spoon the clam and shrimp mixture on top.

PER SERVING (1⅓ cups): 205 Cal, 4 g Fat, 1 g Sat Fat, 0 g Trans Fat, 49 mg Chol, 535 mg Sod, 29 g Carb, 3 g Fib, 15 g Prot, 53 mg Calc. **POINTS** value: **4.**

● ● ●

MEDITERRANEAN-STYLE MIXED SEAFOOD GRILL ✓

prep 30 MIN   *cook* 5 MIN   *serves* 4

2	tablespoons lemon juice
1	tablespoon chopped fresh dill
1	teaspoon dried oregano
1	garlic clove, minced
2	teaspoons olive oil
1	teaspoon Dijon mustard
½	teaspoon salt
8	large sea scallops (about ¾ pound)
1	(½-pound) swordfish or halibut steak, cut into 1-inch chunks
8	large shrimp, peeled and deveined, tails left on if desired
1	fennel bulb, cut into 2-inch chunks
1	red onion, cut into 1½-inch chunks
2	cups hot cooked brown rice

1 Spray the grill rack with olive oil nonstick spray. Preheat the grill to medium-high or prepare a medium-high fire using the direct method (see page 13). If using wooden skewers, soak them in water 30 minutes.

2 Meanwhile, combine the lemon juice, dill, oregano, garlic, oil, mustard, and salt in a large bowl. Add the scallops, swordfish, and shrimp; toss to coat well. Alternately thread the scallops, swordfish, shrimp, fennel, and red onion on 4 (10-inch) skewers.

3 Place the skewers on the grill rack and grill, turning, until the fish is just opaque in the center and the fennel and onion are just tender, 3–4 minutes. Serve with the rice.

PER SERVING (1 skewer and ½ cup rice): 267 Cal, 4 g Fat, 1 g Sat Fat, 0 g Trans Fat, 76 mg Chol, 800 mg Sod, 30 g Carb, 6 g Fib, 26 g Prot, 111 mg Calc. **POINTS** value: **5.**

ARUGULA SALAD WITH
GREMOLATA-TOPPED SCALLOPS

●●●

ARUGULA SALAD WITH GREMOLATA-TOPPED SCALLOPS ☑

prep 30 MIN   *cook* 3 MIN   *serves* 4

¼ cup finely chopped flat-leaf parsley

2 tablespoons grated lime zest

1 garlic clove, minced

3 teaspoons extra-virgin olive oil

½ teaspoon salt

1   pound sea scallops

2 tablespoons lime juice

1 (7-ounce) bag baby arugula

¼ cup thinly sliced red onion

1 Spray the grill rack with olive oil nonstick spray. Preheat the grill to medium-high or prepare a medium-high fire using the direct method (see page 13). Soak 4 (12-inch) wooden skewers in water 30 minutes.

2 Meanwhile, stir together the parsley, lime zest, garlic, 1 teaspoon of the oil, and ¼ teaspoon of the salt in a small bowl; spread on a sheet of wax paper. Coat the scallops with the parsley mixture. Thread one-fourth of the scallops on each of 4 skewers.

3 Place the skewers on the grill rack and grill, turning, until the scallops are just opaque in the center, 2–4 minutes. Transfer to a plate and keep warm.

4 Whisk together the lime juice, the remaining 2 teaspoons oil, and the remaining ¼ teaspoon salt in a large bowl. Add the arugula, tossing to coat evenly. Divide the arugula evenly among 4 plates. Place a skewer on each salad and top with the red onion.

FOOD NOTE

Fresh sea scallops come in two varieties—wet and dry. If possible, avoid buying wet sea scallops. They are chemically treated to extend their shelf life.

PER SERVING (about 3 scallops and 1½ cups salad): 114 Cal, 5 g Fat, 1 g Sat Fat, 0 g Trans Fat, 30 mg Chol, 463 mg Sod, 4 g Carb, 1 g Fib, 15 g Prot, 158 mg Calc. **POINTS** value: **2.**

• • •

TOFU & APPLE SALAD WITH POMEGRANATE VINAIGRETTE

prep 15 MIN   *cook* 15 MIN   *serves* 4

¾ cup pomegranate juice

1 tablespoon packed brown sugar

2 tablespoons red-wine vinegar

1 tablespoon minced shallot

1 tablespoon grated orange zest

2 teaspoons grated lemon zest

2 teaspoons grated peeled fresh ginger

1 teaspoon Asian (dark) sesame oil

¼ teaspoon salt

1 (16-ounce) container extra-firm tofu

1 (4-ounce) bag watercress

1 Granny Smith apple, unpeeled, chopped

1 Spray a vegetable grill topper with nonstick spray and place on the grill rack. Preheat the grill to medium-high or prepare a medium-high fire using the direct method (see page 13).

2 Meanwhile, to make the vinaigrette, combine the pomegranate juice and brown sugar in a small skillet and bring to a boil over medium-high heat. Boil until the mixture is reduced to a syrupy glaze, 6–8 minutes. Transfer the syrup to a medium bowl. Add the vinegar, shallot, orange and lemon zest, ginger, sesame oil, and salt; stir until blended. Set aside.

3 Cut the tofu lengthwise in half and stack the halves; cut crosswise into thirds. Cut each stack on the diagonal to make 12 triangles in all.

4 Place the tofu in a single layer on the grill topper and grill until well marked and heated through, about 3 minutes on each side. Transfer to a plate.

5 Divide the watercress and apple evenly among 4 plates. Top each portion with 3 tofu wedges and drizzle with the vinaigrette.

PER SERVING (2 cups salad, 3 pieces tofu, and 2 tablespoons vinaigrette): 121 Cal, 5 g Fat, 1 g Sat Fat, 0 g Trans Fat, 0 mg Chol, 116 mg Sod, 13 g Carb, 1 g Fib, 8 g Prot, 164 mg Calc. **POINTS** value: **3.**

●●●

GARLICKY EGGPLANT & TEMPEH STIR-FRY

prep 15 MIN   *cook* 15 MIN   *serves* 4

3 tablespoons reduced-sodium chicken broth

2 tablespoons reduced-sodium soy sauce

1 tablespoon balsamic vinegar

1 teaspoon sugar

1 teaspoon Asian (dark) sesame oil

1 teaspoon cornstarch

2 teaspoons canola oil

1 small eggplant (1 pound), cut into 2-inch chunks

1 red bell pepper, cut into thin strips

1 tablespoon minced peeled fresh ginger

2 garlic cloves, minced

1 (8-ounce) package three-grain tempeh, cut into 1½-inch chunks

1 small scallion, thinly sliced

1 Preheat the grill to medium-high or prepare a medium-high fire using the direct method (see page 13).

2 Meanwhile, whisk together the broth, soy sauce, vinegar, sugar, sesame oil, and cornstarch in a small bowl until smooth; set aside.

3 Add the canola oil to a large grill-safe nonstick skillet and place on the grill rack. Add the eggplant and cook, stirring, until almost tender, about 8 minutes. Add the bell pepper, ginger, and garlic. Cook, stirring occasionally, until tender, about 5 minutes. Add the tempeh and toss gently to combine. Re-whisk the broth mixture; add to the skillet and bring to a boil. Reduce the heat and simmer, stirring occasionally, until the sauce bubbles and thickens slightly, about 3 minutes. Sprinkle with the scallion.

PER SERVING (1 cup): 195 Cal, 10 g Fat, 2 g Sat Fat, 0 g Trans Fat, 0 mg Chol, 299 mg Sod, 18 g Carb, 5 g Fib, 12 g Prot, 77 mg Calc. **POINTS** value: **4.**

TRY IT

Tempeh, made from cooked, fermented soybeans, has a firm texture and a nutty flavor. It can be crumbled or cut into small chunks.

CROWD PLEASERS

Chapter 3

● ● ●

CHILI-RUBBED BEEF TENDERLOIN WITH CHUNKY PICO DE GALLO ☑

prep 20 MIN   *cook* 40 MIN   *serves* 12

2   teaspoons chili powder

2   teaspoons ground coriander

1   teaspoon ground cumin

¼   teaspoon salt

¼   teaspoon cayenne

1   (4-pound) center-cut beef tenderloin, trimmed

PICO DE GALLO

1   garlic clove, chopped

¼   teaspoon salt

1   pint grape tomatoes, halved

1   small red onion, finely chopped

¼   cup chopped fresh cilantro

2   fresh or pickled jalapeño peppers, seeded and finely chopped (wear gloves to prevent irritation)

2   teaspoons lime juice

1 Spray the grill rack with olive oil nonstick spray and preheat the grill to medium-high or prepare a medium-high fire using the direct method (see page 13).

2 To make the rub, stir together the chili powder, coriander, cumin, salt, and cayenne in a small bowl. Rub the mixture all over the beef.

3 Place the tenderloin on the grill rack and grill, turning, until browned on all sides, about 10 minutes. Move it to the cooler portion of the grill and grill, covered, turning occasionally, until an instant read thermometer inserted into the center of the tenderloin registers 145°F for medium, 30–35 minutes. Transfer to a cutting board and let stand about 10 minutes.

4 Meanwhile, to make the pico de gallo, with the side of a large knife, mash the garlic with the salt until it forms a paste. Stir together the remaining ingredients with the garlic paste in a serving bowl.

5 Cut the tenderloin into 24 slices and serve with the salsa.

PER SERVING (2 slices beef and generous 2 tablespoons salsa): 191 Cal, 8 g Fat, 3 g Sat Fat, 0 g Trans Fat, 49 mg Chol, 140 mg Sod, 3 g Carb, 1 g Fib, 26 g Prot, 17 mg Calc. ***POINTS*** value: **4.**

CHILI-RUBBED BEEF
TENDERLOIN WITH
CHUNKY PICO DE GALLO
AND GRILLED SMASHED
ROSEMARY POTATOES,
PAGE 154

• • •

ASIAN-STYLE BEEF & LETTUCE PACKAGES

prep 40 MIN   *cook* 50 MIN   *serves* 8

1½ cups long-grain brown rice

¼ teaspoon salt

1 orange bell pepper, cut into ¼-inch strips

1 (2-pound) flank steak, trimmed

¼ teaspoon black pepper

2 tablespoons hoisin sauce

24 small romaine lettuce leaves

24 fresh cilantro sprigs

24 fresh mint sprigs

8 radishes, thinly sliced

8 scallions, thinly sliced

1 tablespoon finely chopped peeled fresh ginger

½ teaspoon sesame seeds

1 Cook the rice with the salt according to the package directions. Stir in the bell pepper; set aside.

2 Meanwhile, spray the grill rack with nonstick spray and preheat the grill to medium-high or prepare a medium-high fire using the direct method (see page 13).

3 Sprinkle the steak with the black pepper. Place on the grill rack and grill, turning, until an instant-read thermometer inserted into the side of the steak registers 145°F for medium, 20–25 minutes, brushing with the hoisin sauce during the last 3 minutes of grilling. Transfer the steak to a cutting board and let stand about 10 minutes.

4 Meanwhile, place the romaine leaves in a pile on a platter and surround with separate piles of the cilantro, mint, and radishes. Stir together the scallions and ginger in a small bowl and add to the platter.

5 Sprinkle the steak with the sesame seeds, then cut across the grain into 24 slices. Pile the steak and rice in separate serving bowls. Have diners assemble their own packages by filling each lettuce leaf with ⅔ cup rice, 1 slice steak, 1 cilantro sprig, 1 mint sprig, a few radish slices, and a sprinkling of the scallion mixture. Roll or fold up the lettuce packets and eat out of hand.

HOW WE DID IT

To clean a grill, use our favorite method. Ball up a piece of foil and grasp it with tongs. Use the foil ball to scrape the rack clean.

PER SERVING (3 packages): 326 Cal, 9 g Fat, 3 g Sat Fat, 0 g Trans Fat, 46 mg Chol, 507 mg Sod, 32 g Carb, 5 g Fib, 29 g Prot, 48 mg Calc. **POINTS** value: **6.**

● ● ●

BEEF BRISKET WITH FETA CHIMICHURRI SAUCE

prep 20 MIN   *cook* 40 MIN   *serves* 8

2   garlic cloves, finely chopped

¼   teaspoon salt

1   tablespoon finely chopped
     fresh oregano

¼   teaspoon cayenne

1   (2-pound) first-cut brisket,
     trimmed

FETA CHIMICHURRI SAUCE

½   cup chopped flat-leaf
     parsley

3   tablespoons chopped
     fresh cilantro

2   tablespoons chopped
     fresh basil

1   tablespoon olive oil

1   tablespoon red-wine
     vinegar

1   fresh or pickled jalapeño
     pepper, seeded and minced
     (wear gloves to prevent
     irritation)

2   tablespoons crumbled
     reduced-fat feta cheese

1 With the side of a large knife, mash the garlic and salt until it forms a paste. Stir together the garlic paste with the oregano, and cayenne in a cup; rub all over the brisket. Place in a large zip-close plastic bag. Squeeze out the air and seal the bag. Refrigerate at least 4 hours or up to 6 hours.

2 Meanwhile, spray the grill rack with nonstick spray and preheat the grill to medium-high or prepare a medium-high fire using the direct method (see page 13).

3 Remove the brisket from the bag. Place on the grill rack and grill, turning occasionally, until an instant-read thermometer inserted into the center of the meat registers 145°F for medium, about 40 minutes. Transfer to a cutting board and let stand about 10 minutes.

4 Meanwhile, to make the chimichurri sauce, stir together all of the ingredients except the feta cheese in a serving bowl. Stir in the feta.

5 Cut the brisket across the grain into 32 slices. Serve with the chimichurri sauce.

PER SERVING (about 4 slices beef and about 1 tablespoon sauce): 162 Cal, 8 g Fat, 3 g Sat Fat, 0 g Trans Fat, 40 mg Chol, 129 mg Sod, 1 g Carb, 0 g Fib, 20 g Prot, 26 mg Calc. **POINTS** value: **4.**

FAJITAS WITH GUACAMOLE & SALSA

FAJITAS WITH GUACAMOLE & SALSA

prep 25 MIN   *cook* 25 MIN   *serves* 6

- 2 yellow and/or orange bell peppers
- 2 small red onions, halved through the root end
- 1 (1-pound) top round steak, trimmed
- 1 Hass avocado, pitted, peeled, and cut into ½-inch pieces
- 2 tomatoes, seeded and cut into ½-inch pieces
- 2 tablespoons finely chopped white onion
- ½ teaspoon grated lime zest
- 2 teaspoons lime juice
- ½ teaspoon salt
- ⅛ teaspoon cayenne
- ¼ cup lightly packed fresh cilantro leaves
- 6 (9-inch) flour tortillas, warmed
- 1 cup salsa, such as Tomato-Chipotle Salsa (page 39)

1 Spray the grill rack with nonstick spray and preheat the grill to medium-high or prepare a medium-high fire using the direct method (see page 13).

2 Place the bell peppers and red onions on the grill rack and grill until the peppers are blackened on all sides and the onions are browned and beginning to soften, about 15 minutes. Transfer the peppers to a large zip-close plastic bag and seal the bag; let steam 10 minutes.

3 Meanwhile, place the steak on the grill rack and grill, turning, until an instant-read thermometer inserted into the center of the steak registers 145°F for medium, 12–15 minutes. Transfer to a cutting board and let stand about 10 minutes.

4 When cool enough to handle, peel and seed the peppers, then cut into ½-inch strips. Slice the onions, then combine with the peppers in a medium bowl.

5 To make the guacamole, combine the avocado, half of the tomatoes, the white onion, lime zest and juice, ¼ teaspoon of the salt, and half of the cayenne in a serving bowl.

6 Cut the beef across the grain into ¼-inch slices. Add the beef to the bell pepper–onion mixture; stir in the remaining tomato, the cilantro, the remaining ¼ teaspoon salt, and the cayenne. Pile the beef mixture in the tortillas. Serve with the guacamole and salsa.

PER SERVING (1 tortilla, ¾ cup beef filling, ¼ cup guacamole, and generous 2 tablespoons salsa): 355 Cal, 11 g Fat, 2 g Sat Fat, 0 g Trans Fat, 39 mg Chol, 849 mg Sod, 42 g Carb, 5 g Fib, 23 g Prot, 107 mg Calc. **POINTS** value: **7.**

• • •

GRILLED PORK, ORANGE
& RED ONION SALAD ✓

prep 25 MIN *cook* 20 MIN *serves* 8

¼ cup red-wine vinegar

2 tablespoons extra-virgin olive oil

2 shallots, finely chopped

2 garlic cloves, finely chopped

2 teaspoons chopped fresh tarragon or ½ teaspoon dried

2 teaspoons Dijon mustard

½ teaspoon salt

¼ teaspoon black pepper

2 (1-pound) pork tenderloins, trimmed

2 large heads romaine lettuce, cut crosswise into 1-inch pieces

6 navel oranges, peeled and cut into sections

1 red onion, thinly sliced

1 Spray the grill rack with olive oil nonstick spray and preheat the grill to medium-high or prepare a medium-high fire using the direct method (see page 13).

2 Meanwhile, to make the dressing, whisk together the vinegar, oil, shallots, garlic, tarragon, mustard, salt, and pepper in a small bowl.

3 Place the tenderloins on the grill rack and grill, turning, until an instant-read thermometer inserted into the center of the meat registers 160°F for medium, about 20 minutes, Transfer to a cutting board and let stand about 10 minutes. Cut the pork into ¼-inch slices.

4 Combine the pork, romaine, orange segments, and red onion in a serving bowl. Drizzle with the dressing and toss to coat evenly.

PER SERVING (3 cups): 278 Cal, 8 g Fat, 2 g Sat Fat, 0 g Trans Fat, 67 mg Chol, 240 mg Sod, 25 g Carb, 7 g Fib, 28 g Prot, 123 mg Calc. ***POINTS*** value: **5.**

● ● ●

ASIAN-STYLE SPARERIBS WITH GINGER DIPPING SAUCE

prep 30 MIN   *cook* 1 HR 35 MIN   *serves* 12

RIBS

1½ teaspoons packed brown sugar

½ teaspoon Chinese five-spice powder

½ teaspoon ground coriander

½ teaspoon salt

¼ teaspoon black pepper

1 (12-rib) rack spareribs (about 2 pounds)

⅓ cup apricot jam, warmed

GINGER DIPPING SAUCE

½ cup apricot jam

¼ cup minced peeled fresh ginger

¼ cup reduced-sodium soy sauce

2 tablespoons unseasoned rice vinegar

¼ teaspoon crushed red pepper

1 Preheat the oven to 300°F.

2 To make the rub for the ribs, combine the brown sugar, five-spice powder, coriander, salt, and black pepper in a cup. Rub on both sides of the ribs. Place the ribs in a large roasting pan and cover tightly with foil. Bake until fork-tender, about 1½ hours.

3 Meanwhile, spray the grill rack with nonstick spray and preheat the grill to high or prepare a hot fire using the direct method (see page 13).

4 To make the ginger dipping sauce, combine all the ingredients in a small saucepan and bring just to a simmer. Transfer to a serving bowl; keep warm.

5 Place the ribs on the grill rack and grill, turning frequently and basting with the apricot jam until well marked, 5–7 minutes. Cut the rack into individual ribs and arrange on a platter. Serve with the dipping sauce.

PER SERVING (1 rib and scant 1 tablespoon sauce): 155 Cal, 9 g Fat, 3 g Sat Fat, 0 g Trans Fat, 36 mg Chol, 280 mg Sod, 9 g Carb, 0 g Fib, 9 g Prot, 20 mg Calc. **POINTS** value: **4.**

ZAP IT

Make the ginger dipping sauce a day ahead and refrigerate in a covered microwavable container. Reheat in the microwave on High for about 1 minute.

●●●

MAPLE-BRINED PORK CHOPS WITH BASIL-STUFFED NECTARINES

prep 25 MIN   *cook* 10 MIN   *serves* 6

2½ quarts water

1   cup pure maple syrup

¾   cup kosher salt

6   (6-ounce) pork rib chops, trimmed

7   small nectarines, halved

6   fresh basil leaves, finely chopped

Pinch grated lime zest

2   teaspoons lime juice

Pinch black pepper

1 Stir together the water, ¾ cup of the maple syrup, and the salt in a large pot until the salt is dissolved. Add the pork chops and refrigerate, covered, for at least 4 hours or up to 6 hours.

2 Meanwhile, spray the grill rack with nonstick spray and preheat the grill to medium-high or prepare a medium-high fire using the direct method (see page 13).

3 Remove the pork chops from the brine; rinse well under cold running water, then pat dry with paper towels. Place the pork chops on the grill rack and grill, brushing with the remaining ¼ cup maple syrup, until well marked and cooked through, 3–5 minutes on each side. At the same time, place 12 of the nectarine halves, cut side down, on the grill rack and grill until lightly browned and beginning to soften, about 4 minutes on each side.

4 Finely chop the remaining 2 nectarine halves. Stir together the chopped nectarines, basil, lime zest and juice, and pepper in a small bowl. Spoon about 1½ teaspoons of the basil mixture into each nectarine half. Serve with the pork.

PER SERVING (1 pork chop and 2 filled nectarine halves): 281 Cal, 10 g Fat, 3 g Sat Fat, 0 g Trans Fat, 76 mg Chol, 1180 mg Sod, 21 g Carb, 1 g Fib, 27 g Prot, 25 mg Calc. **POINTS** value: **6.**

MAPLE-BRINED PORK CHOPS WITH
BASIL-STUFFED NECTARINES

• • •

TANDOORI-MARINATED
BUTTERFLIED LEG OF LAMB

prep 20 MIN   *cook* 25 MIN   *serves* 8

¾   cup plain fat-free yogurt

1½   teaspoons finely chopped
      peeled fresh ginger

2   large garlic cloves, finely
      chopped

¾   teaspoon paprika

½   teaspoon ground cumin

¼   teaspoon ground cardamom

¼   teaspoon cayenne

1   (2-pound) butterflied
      boneless leg of lamb,
      trimmed

¼   teaspoon salt

1   cup whole-wheat couscous

⅓   cup coarsely chopped
      pistachios or toasted sliced
      almonds

½   cup dried currants

1 Combine the yogurt, ginger, garlic, paprika, cumin, cardamom, and cayenne in a large bowl; set aside.

2 Lay the lamb flat on a work surface and gently pound with a meat mallet or rolling pin until an even thickness. Add the lamb to the yogurt mixture and spread it all over the lamb. Cover and refrigerate at least 1 hour or up to 3 hours.

3 Spray the grill rack with nonstick spray and preheat the grill to medium-high or prepare a medium-high fire using the direct method (see page 13).

4 Wipe off the excess yogurt mixture from the lamb; sprinkle the lamb with ⅛ teaspoon of the salt. Place the lamb on the grill rack and grill, turning, until an instant-read thermometer inserted into the thickest part of the lamb registers 145°F for medium, about 25 minutes. Transfer to a cutting board and let stand about 10 minutes.

5 Meanwhile, cook the couscous according to the package directions using the remaining ⅛ teaspoon salt. Transfer to a serving bowl and stir in the pistachios and currants.

6 Cut the lamb across the grain into 32 slices. Serve with the couscous.

FOOD NOTE

It is important not to marinate the lamb longer than 3 hours, as the acid in the yogurt could give the meat a mushy texture.

PER SERVING (4 slices lamb and scant ½ cup couscous): 296 Cal, 11 g Fat, 3 g Sat Fat, 0 g Trans Fat, 79 mg Chol, 154 mg Sod, 21 g Carb, 3 g Fib, 29 g Prot, 78 mg Calc. **POINTS** value: **6.**

CHICKEN WITH ORANGE & BASIL GREMOLATA

prep 25 MIN   *cook* 20 MIN   *serves* 8

1   large naval orange

4   small garlic cloves

½   teaspoon salt

1½ cups orange juice

¼   cup lemon juice

½   cup thinly sliced fresh basil
     + 4 leaves

2   (1-inch pieces) cinnamon
     stick, broken in half

⅛   teaspoon cayenne

2   (3-pound) chickens, cut into
     quarters, wings and skin
     removed

1 Grate ½ teaspoon zest from the orange; set aside. With a vegetable peeler, remove the remaining zest in strips. With the side of a large knife, mash 2 of the garlic cloves with the salt until it forms a paste.

2 Combine the orange juice, lemon juice, strips of orange zest, the garlic paste, sliced basil, cinnamon pieces, and cayenne in a 2-gallon zip-close plastic bag and add the chicken. Squeeze out the air and seal the bag; turn to coat the chicken. Refrigerate, turning the bag occasionally, at least 2 hours or up to 6 hours.

3 Meanwhile, spray the grill rack with nonstick spray and preheat the grill to medium-high or prepare a medium-high fire using the direct method (see page 13).

4 Remove the chicken from the marinade; discard the marinade. Place the chicken on the grill rack and grill, turning, until cooked through, 18–20 minutes.

5 To make the gremolata, finely chop together the remaining 2 garlic cloves and the 4 basil leaves; add the grated orange zest. Transfer the chicken to a platter and sprinkle with the gremolata.

PER SERVING (1 chicken quarter): 240 Cal, 9 g Fat, 2 g Sat Fat, 0 g Trans Fat, 108 mg Chol, 141 mg Sod, 2 g Carb, 0 g Fib, 35 g Prot, 25 mg Calc. ***POINTS*** value: **6.**

GRILLED LAMB KOFTA

● ● ●

GRILLED LAMB KOFTA ☑

prep 20 MIN   *cook* 10 MIN   *serves* 6

2 pounds ground lean lamb
   (preferably ground 2 times)

4 scallions (white part only)
   finely chopped

⅓ cup finely chopped
   fresh cilantro

1 egg white, lightly beaten

2 teaspoons ground cumin

1 teaspoon dried thyme

1 teaspoon ground allspice

½ teaspoon salt

¼ teaspoon black pepper

1 cup plain fat-free yogurt

2 cups lightly packed
   shredded romaine lettuce

3 plum tomatoes, thinly sliced

1 Mix together the lamb, half of the scallions, the cilantro, egg white, cumin, thyme, allspice, salt, and pepper in a large bowl until thoroughly combined. With your hands, knead the mixture thoroughly (or with a wooden spoon, press the mixture against the side of the bowl). Cover tightly and refrigerate about 1 hour.

2 Meanwhile, if using wooden skewers, soak 12 (12-inch) wooden skewers in water 30 minutes.

3 With damp hands, shape the lamb mixture into 12 (1 x 4-inch) sausage shapes. Thread the lamb koftas lengthwise on the skewers, then taper the ends of each kofta. Refrigerate, covered, until ready to grill or up to 8 hours.

4 Stir together the yogurt and the remaining scallions. Set aside at room temperature up to 2 hours or refrigerate up to 6 hours.

5 Spray the grill rack with olive oil nonstick spray and preheat the grill to medium-high or prepare a medium-high fire using the direct method (see page 13).

6 Place the skewers on the grill rack and grill, turning, until the lamb is evenly browned and cooked through, about 10 minutes. Divide the lettuce evenly among 6 plates and top with the tomatoes and koftas. Serve with the yogurt dipping sauce.

PER SERVING (2 koftas, ½ tomato, ⅓ cup lettuce, and scant 3 tablespoons sauce): 224 Cal, 9 g Fat, 3 g Sat Fat, 0 g Trans Fat, 84 mg Chol, 307 mg Sod, 6 g Carb, 1 g Fib, 29 g Prot, 111 mg Calc. **POINTS** value: **5.**

● ● ●

ALL-AMERICAN BBQ CHICKEN

prep 25 MIN   *cook* 35 MIN   *serves* 6

1 cup hickory chips

1 cup ketchup

⅔ cup strong brewed coffee

½ cup packed brown sugar

¼ cup apple-cider vinegar

¼ cup chopped flat-leaf parsley

1 garlic clove, crushed with the side of a large knife

1 teaspoon salt

¼ teaspoon crushed red pepper

6 bone-in chicken breast halves, skinned

TRY IT

A barbecue sauce is made even better with the addition of strongly brewed coffee. The coffee cuts the sauce's sweetness and contributes deep, rich flavor.

1 Spray the grill rack with nonstick spray. Preheat the grill to medium-high or prepare a medium-high fire using the indirect method (see page 13). Soak the hickory chips in water 30 minutes.

2 Meanwhile, combine the ketchup, coffee, brown sugar, vinegar, parsley, garlic, ½ teaspoon of the salt, and the crushed red pepper in a medium saucepan and set over medium heat. Cook, stirring, until the sugar is dissolved, about 3 minutes. Bring the mixture to a boil, then reduce the heat and simmer, about 10 minutes. Pour through a strainer set over a bowl; let cool to room temperature.

3 Sprinkle the chicken with the remaining ½ teaspoon salt. If using a gas grill, spread the chips in a small disposable foil pan with a few holes poked in and set on top of a lit burner. If using a charcoal grill, scatter the chips over the coals. Place the chicken, meaty side down, on the cooler portion of the grill rack and grill, covered, turning once or twice, 15 minutes. Uncover the grill and continue to grill the chicken, brushing with the remaining sauce, until cooked through, about 5 minutes.

PER SERVING (1 chicken breast half): 233 Cal, 4 g Fat, 1 g Sat Fat, 0 g Trans Fat, 73 mg Chol, 703 mg Sod, 21 g Carb, 0 g Fib, 27 g Prot, 34 mg Calc. ***POINTS*** value: **5.**

ALL-AMERICAN BBQ CHICKEN
AND MEXICAN GRILLED CORN,
PAGE 142

● ● ●

PAELLA SALAD WITH CHICKEN & SHRIMP SKEWERS ✓

prep 35 MIN   *cook* 50 MIN   *serves* 6

1   cup long-grain brown rice

¾   teaspoon salt

¼   teaspoon saffron threads, finely crumbled

1   fennel bulb, trimmed, cored, and cut into long, thin strips

1   yellow bell pepper, thinly sliced

1   plum tomato, seeded and cut into ½-inch pieces

½   cup frozen peas, thawed

¼   cup + 2 tablespoons chopped flat-leaf parsley

1   tablespoon + 2 teaspoons olive oil

2   teaspoons grated lemon zest

3   tablespoons lemon juice

¼   teaspoon + ⅛ teaspoon black pepper

2   skinless boneless chicken breast halves

36   medium shrimp (1 pound), peeled and deveined

1 To make the rice salad, cook the rice according to the package directions using ¼ teaspoon of the salt and the saffron. Transfer the rice to a large bowl and stir in the fennel, bell pepper, tomato, peas, ¼ cup of the parsley, 1 tablespoon of the oil, the lemon zest, 1 tablespoon of the lemon juice, ¼ teaspoon of the salt, and ¼ teaspoon of the black pepper. Set aside.

2 Spray the grill rack with olive oil nonstick spray and preheat the grill to medium-high or prepare a medium-high fire using the direct method (see page 13). Soak 18 (12-inch) wooden skewers in water 30 minutes.

3 Separate the tenders from the chicken breast halves; set aside. Cut each breast half on the diagonal into 5 strips. Whisk together the remaining 2 tablespoons lemon juice, the remaining 2 teaspoons oil, the remaining ¼ teaspoon salt, and ⅛ teaspoon black pepper in a large bowl. Add the chicken breast strips, chicken tenders, and shrimp; toss to coat evenly. Let stand at room temperature 15 minutes.

4 Thread 1 piece of chicken on each of 12 skewers and 6 shrimp on each of 6 skewers.

5 Place the skewers on the grill rack and grill, turning, until the chicken is cooked through and the shrimp until just opaque in the center, 8–10 minutes. Spoon the rice salad on each of 6 plates; top each with 2 chicken skewers and 1 shrimp skewer and sprinkle with the remaining 2 tablespoons parsley.

PER SERVING (2 chicken skewers, 1 shrimp skewer, and scant 1 cup rice salad): 258 Cal, 7 g Fat, 1 g Sat Fat, 0 g Trans Fat, 82 mg Chol, 250 mg Sod, 31 g Carb, 6 g Fib, 19 g Prot, 58 mg Calc. **POINTS** value: **5.**

●●●

CHILI-RUBBED TURKEY BREAST

prep 10 MIN   *cook* 1 HR 30 MIN   *serves* 10

2   cups mesquite chips

1   tablespoon chili powder

1   tablespoon salt

1   tablespoon packed
    brown sugar

2   teaspoons ground cumin

1   teaspoon paprika

1   teaspoon garlic powder

1   (5½- to 6-pound) turkey
    breast

1 Remove the grill rack from the grill. Preheat the grill to medium-high or prepare a medium-high fire using the indirect method (see page 13). Soak the mesquite chips in water 30 minutes.

2 To make the rub, combine all the ingredients except the turkey in a small bowl. Spread the rub all over the turkey breast, then place the turkey in a disposable foil roasting pan.

3 If using a gas grill, put the mesquite chips in a disposable foil loaf pan with a few holes poked in and set on top of a lit burner; return the grill rack to the grill. If using a charcoal grill scatter the chips over the coals.

4 Place the pan with the turkey on the cooler portion of the grill rack and grill, covered, until an instant-read thermometer inserted into the thickest part of the breast registers 170°F, about 1½ hours. If any parts of the skin brown too quickly, cover them with foil.

5 Transfer the turkey to a cutting board and let stand about 10 minutes. Carve the meat. Remove the skin before eating.

PER SERVING (2 slices turkey): 223 Cal, 2 g Fat, 1 g Sat Fat, 0 g Trans Fat, 130 mg Chol, 801 mg Sod, 2 g Carb, 0 g Fib, 46 g Prot, 31 mg Calc. **POINTS** value: **5**.

GARLIC & HERB–RUBBED TURKEY
AND GRILL–ROASTED FALL
VEGETABLES, PAGE 164

●●●

GARLIC & HERB–RUBBED TURKEY ☑

prep 15 MIN   *cook* 2 HR 15 MIN   *serves* 12

3 garlic cloves, chopped

2 teaspoons salt

2 tablespoons chopped
   fresh rosemary

2 tablespoons chopped
   fresh sage

¾ teaspoon black pepper

1 (12-pound) turkey, giblets
   removed

3 fresh rosemary sprigs

3 fresh sage sprigs

1 Spray a V-rack with olive oil nonstick spray and place in a disposable foil roasting pan. Preheat the grill to high or prepare a hot fire using the indirect method (see page 13).

2 Meanwhile, with the side of a large knife, mash the garlic with 1 teaspoon of the salt until it forms a paste. Combine the garlic paste with the chopped rosemary, chopped sage, and ½ teaspoon of the pepper in a small bowl. Using your fingers, carefully loosen the skin on the turkey breast and spread the herb mixture on the meat under the skin; press the skin back into place. Fold the neck skin underneath and tuck the wing tips under. Sprinkle the remaining 1 teaspoon salt and ¼ teaspoon pepper in the turkey cavity; add the rosemary and sage sprigs. Tie the legs together with kitchen string.

3 Put the turkey on the V-rack and add 2 cups water to the pan. If using a gas grill, set the pan over the turned-off burner; if using a charcoal grill, place the turkey on the cooler portion of the grill rack. Grill, covered, until an instant-read thermometer inserted into the thickest part of a thigh registers 180°F, about 2½ hours, adjusting the temperature if needed to maintain 400°F and rotating the pan after 1 hour. If the skin browns too quickly, cover it with foil.

4 Transfer the turkey to a cutting board and let stand 10 minutes. Discard the herb sprigs. Carve the meat. Remove the skin before eating.

PER SERVING (2 slices white meat or 1 slice dark meat): 127 Cal, 2 g Fat, 1 g Sat Fat, 0 g Trans Fat, 81 mg Chol, 196 mg Sod, 0 g Carb, 0 g Fib, 25 g Prot, 20 mg Calc.
POINTS value: *3.*

●●●

SALMON WITH EDAMAME SALAD ☑

prep 20 MIN   *cook* 20 MIN   *Serves* 6

1   (1-pound) bag frozen shelled edamame, thawed

2   plum tomatoes, seeded and cut into ½-inch dice

3   scallions, thinly sliced

2   tablespoons lime juice

½   teaspoon salt

¼   teaspoon black pepper

1½   teaspoons ground coriander

6   (¼-pound) skinless salmon fillets

¼   cup coarsely chopped fresh cilantro

6   lime wedges

1 To make the edamame salad, cook the edamame according to the package directions. Drain in a colander, then hold under cold running water to stop the cooking; drain again. Stir together the edamame, tomatoes, scallions, lime juice, ¼ teaspoon of the salt, and ⅛ teaspoon of the pepper in a large bowl. Let stand at room temperature up to 1 hour.

2 Meanwhile, spray the grill rack with olive oil nonstick spray. Preheat the grill to medium-high or prepare a medium-high fire using the direct method (see page 13).

3 Stir together the coriander and the remaining ¼ teaspoon salt and ⅛ teaspoon pepper in a cup; rub all over the salmon.

4 Place the salmon on the grill rack and grill until just opaque in the center, 2–3 minutes on each side. Place a fillet on each of 6 plates and spoon the edamame salad alongside. Sprinkle with the cilantro and garnish each serving with a lime wedge.

GOOD IDEA
You can also make the salad with delicious fresh fava beans instead of the edamame. You will need about 4 pounds of fava beans in the pod to yield 4 cups of beans.

PER SERVING (1 salmon fillet and ⅔ cup salad): 278 Cal, 11 g Fat, 2 g Sat Fat, 0 g Trans Fat, 75 mg Chol, 278 mg Sod, 11 g Carb, 4 g Fib, 34 g Prot, 136 mg Calc. **POINTS** value: **6.**

• • •

ROSEMARY-GRILLED SALMON ☑

prep 15 MIN   *cook* 10 MIN   *serves* 6

2 teaspoons grated lemon zest

¼ cup lemon juice

1 tablespoon olive oil

2 teaspoons chopped fresh rosemary

½ teaspoon salt

⅛ teaspoon black pepper

6 (6-ounce) salmon steaks, 1-inch thick

6 fresh rosemary sprigs

6 (¼-inch) lemon slices

1 Stir together the lemon zest and juice, oil, chopped rosemary, salt, and pepper in a small bowl. Put the salmon on a platter and drizzle on both sides with the lemon juice mixture; refrigerate about 15 minutes.

2 Meanwhile, spray the grill rack with olive oil nonstick spray and preheat the grill to medium-high or prepare a medium-high fire using the direct method (see page 13).

3 With tongs, push 3 of the rosemary sprigs through the grill rack. Place the salmon steaks and lemon slices on the grill rack and grill until the fish is just opaque in the center and the lemon slices are lightly charred along the edges, 4–5 minutes on each side. Transfer the salmon to a platter and garnish with the lemon slices and the remaining 3 rosemary sprigs.

PER SERVING (1 salmon steak): 230 Cal, 11 g Fat, 3 g Sat Fat, 0 g Trans Fat, 95 mg Chol, 285 mg Sod, 1 g Carb, 0 g Fib, 31 g Prot, 22 mg Calc. **POINTS** value: **6.**

●●●

MISO-RUBBED HALIBUT WITH CELLOPHANE NOODLE SALAD

prep 25 MIN   *cook* 10 MIN   *serves* 6

6   cups boiling water

6   ounces cellophane noodles
     (bean thread vermicelli)

1   small red or yellow bell
     pepper, cut into ¼-inch dice

3   scallions, thinly sliced

⅓   cup lightly packed fresh
     cilantro leaves

1   fresh or pickled jalapeño
     pepper, seeded and finely
     chopped (wear gloves to
     prevent irritation)

¼   cup seasoned rice vinegar

3   tablespoons white miso

3   tablespoons packed
     brown sugar

6   (6-ounce) halibut steaks,
     about 1 inch thick

1 Spray the grill rack with nonstick spray and preheat the grill to medium or prepare a medium fire using the direct method (see page 13).

2 Meanwhile, to make the noodle salad, pour the boiling water over the noodles in a large bowl and let stand until softened, about 4 minutes. Drain in a colander, then rinse under cold running water; drain again. Transfer the noodles to a large bowl and add the bell pepper, scallions, cilantro, jalapeño, and vinegar, tossing to mix well; set aside.

3 Stir together the miso and brown sugar in a small bowl; spread over both sides of the halibut. Place on the grill rack and grill until the fish is just opaque in the center, about 5 minutes on each side. Transfer a steak to each of 6 plates and spoon the noodle salad alongside.

PER SERVING (1 halibut steak and ⅔ cup noodle salad): 319 Cal, 2 g Fat, 1 g Sat Fat, 0 g Trans Fat, 74 mg Chol, 622 mg Sod, 43 g Carb, 2 g Fib, 29 g Prot, 42 mg Calc. **POINTS** value: **6.**

●●●

JERK RED SNAPPER WITH PINEAPPLE ☑

prep 20 MIN   *cook* 10 MIN   *serves* 6

3   (½-pound) red snapper fillets

1½ teaspoons jerk seasoning
    without added sugar

6   (½-inch) slices fresh
    pineapple, cored

¾   teaspoon ground coriander

Pinch cayenne

1 Spray the grill rack with olive oil nonstick spray and preheat the grill to medium or prepare a medium fire using the direct method (see page 13).

2 Sprinkle the red snapper with the jerk seasoning and sprinkle the pineapple slices with the coriander and cayenne. Place the fish and pineapple on the grill rack and grill until the fish is just opaque throughout and the pineapple is well marked and softened, about 4 minutes on each side.

3 Transfer the fish to a cutting board and cut each fillet crosswise in half. Transfer a pineapple slice to each of 6 plates. Place a piece of fish on each plate.

PER SERVING (½ snapper fillet and 1 pineapple slice): 133 Cal, 2 g Fat, 0 g Sat Fat, 0 g Trans Fat, 60 mg Chol, 94 mg Sod, 8 g Carb, 1 g Fib, 22 g Prot, 28 mg Calc. **POINTS** value: **3.**

• • •

GLAZED SHRIMP SKEWERS WITH ASIAN SLAW

prep 35 MIN   *cook* 8 MIN   *serves* 6

4 cups finely shredded red cabbage

3 carrots, cut into matchstick strips

¾ cup seasoned rice vinegar

1 tablespoon minced peeled fresh ginger

¼ teaspoon crushed red pepper

24 jumbo shrimp (about 1½ pounds), peeled and deveined, tails left on if desired

3 tablespoons mild molasses

2 tablespoons finely chopped dry-roasted peanuts

1 tablespoon thinly sliced fresh mint

Small mint leaves (optional)

1 To make the slaw, combine the cabbage, carrots, vinegar, ginger, and crushed red pepper in a large zip-close plastic bag. Squeeze out the air and seal the bag; turn to coat the vegetables. Refrigerate at least 2 hours or up to overnight, turning the bag occasionally.

2 Meanwhile, spray the grill rack with nonstick spray and preheat the grill to medium-high or prepare a medium-high fire using the direct method (see page 13). Soak 6 (12-inch) wooden skewers in water 30 minutes.

3 Thread 4 shrimp on each skewer, leaving a small space between each one.

4 Place the skewers on the grill rack and grill until the shrimp are just opaque in the center, 2–4 minutes on each side. Let cool slightly, then lightly brush with the molasses and sprinkle with the peanuts.

5 With a slotted spoon, transfer the slaw to each of 6 plates. Place a shrimp skewer on top of each salad and sprinkle with mint leaves if using.

PER SERVING (1 skewer and 1 cup slaw): 158 Cal, 2 g Fat, 0 g Sat Fat, 0 g Trans Fat, 78 mg Chol, 633 mg Sod, 26 g Carb, 2 g Fib, 10 g Prot, 72 mg Calc. **POINTS** value: **3.**

GLAZED SHRIMP SKEWERS
WITH ASIAN SLAW

SCALLOPS WITH TOMATO-ONION SALSA

prep 25 MIN   *cook* 5 MIN   *serves* 6

4   tomatoes, seeded and cut into ¼-inch dice

1   small red onion, cut into ¼-inch dice

2   tablespoons finely chopped chives

4   basil leaves, thinly sliced

1   tablespoon balsamic vinegar

1   tablespoon olive oil

½   teaspoon salt

¼   teaspoon black pepper

2   pounds sea scallops

1 To make the salsa, gently stir together the tomatoes, red onion, chives, basil, vinegar, oil, ¼ teaspoon of the salt, and ⅛ teaspoon of the pepper in a medium bowl. Cover and let stand at room temperature up to 1 hour.

2 Meanwhile, spray the grill rack with olive oil nonstick spray and preheat the grill to medium-high or prepare a medium-high fire using the direct method (see page 13). Soak 12 (12-inch) wooden skewers in water 30 minutes.

3 Thread 2 parallel skewers through about 6 scallops, holding the skewers about ½ inch apart. Repeat with the remaining scallops and sprinkle with the remaining ¼ teaspoon salt and ⅛ teaspoon pepper.

4 Place the skewers on the grill rack and grill the scallops, turning, until just opaque in the center, 6–8 minutes. Slide the scallops off the skewers and divide evenly among 6 plates. Top evenly with the salsa.

HOW WE DID IT

A step as simple as separating the scallops a bit on the skewers ensures that they cook quickly and evenly.

PER SERVING (about 6 scallops and ⅓ cup salsa): 125 Cal, 3 g Fat, 0 g Sat Fat, 0 g Trans Fat, 40 mg Chol, 402 mg Sod, 5 g Carb, 1 g Fib, 18 g Prot, 100 mg Calc. **POINTS** value: **3.**

●●●

CREMINI MUSHROOM & BROWN RICE BURGERS

prep 15 MIN   *cook* 20 MIN   *serves* 6

1 (8-ounce) package sliced cremini mushrooms

1 onion, chopped

¼ cup water

1 tablespoon reduced-sodium soy sauce

1 (8.5 ounce) package prepared whole-grain brown and wild rice blend

¼ cup plain dried bread crumbs

¼ cup shredded fat-free mozzarella cheese

1 egg white

6 whole-wheat hamburger buns, split

6 lettuce leaves

6 tomato slices

1 Spray a large nonstick skillet with nonstick spray and set over medium-high heat. Add the mushrooms, onion, water, and soy sauce; bring to a boil. Reduce the heat and simmer, covered, until the liquid evaporates and the mushrooms and onion are tender, about 8 minutes.

2 Transfer the mushroom mixture to a food processor; pulse until smooth, then transfer to a large bowl. Add the rice blend, bread crumbs, mozzarella, and egg white; stir until blended. Cover and refrigerate at least 1 hour or up to 24 hours.

3 Meanwhile, preheat the grill to medium-high or prepare a medium-high fire using the direct method (see page 13).

4 With damp hands, shape the mixture into 6 (¾-inch-thick) patties.

5 Spray a vegetable grill topper with nonstick spray and place on the grill rack. Place the patties on the topper and grill until the patties are browned and heated through, 4–6 minutes on each side. Place the buns, cut side down, on the grill rack and grill until toasted, 2–3 minutes.

6 Place the burgers on the bottoms of the buns and top with the lettuce and tomato. Replace the tops of the buns.

PER SERVING (1 burger): 201 Cal, 3 g Fat, 1 g Sat Fat, 0 g Trans Fat, 1 mg Chol, 635 mg Sod, 37 g Carb, 5 g Fib, 10 g Prot, 95 mg Calc. **POINTS** value: **3.**

PACKET GRILLING

Chapter 4

●●●

FILET MIGNON WITH APRICOT-ORANGE SAUCE

prep 15 MIN   *cook* 10 MIN   *serves* 4

4 ripe apricots, halved, pitted, and sliced

¼ cup sweet orange marmalade

2 tablespoons thinly sliced scallion

1 jalapeño pepper, seeded and minced (wear gloves to prevent irritation)

2 teaspoons olive oil

2 tablespoons orange juice

4 (¼-pound) filets mignons, ½ inch thick, trimmed

1 garlic clove, minced

½ teaspoon salt

⅛ teaspoon black pepper

2 tablespoons chopped fresh cilantro

1 Preheat the grill to medium-high or prepare a medium-high fire using the direct method (see page 13). Tear off 4 (15 x 18-inch) sheets of heavy-duty foil and spray the centers with nonstick spray.

2 Gently toss together the apricots, marmalade, scallion, jalapeño, and oil in a medium bowl. Place one-fourth of the mixture in the center of each foil sheet and drizzle evenly with the orange juice. Sprinkle the filets with the garlic, salt, and pepper; place a filet on top of each portion of the apricot mixture.

3 To close the packets, bring the two opposite long sides of the foil up to meet in the center; fold the edges over twice, making ½-inch-wide folds, to seal tightly. Double-fold the open sides, making ½-inch-wide folds, to seal tightly.

4 Place the packets on the grill rack and grill, covered, until the beef is medium done, about 10 minutes. With a wide spatula, transfer the packets to a cutting board; carefully open, standing back to avoid the steam. Transfer the beef and apricot mixture to each of 4 plates; drizzle with the juices and sprinkle with the cilantro.

GOOD IDEA

If apricots aren't in season, substitute 8 well-drained canned apricot halves packed in light syrup.

PER SERVING (1 filet and ½ cup apricot mixture): 279 Cal, 10 g Fat, 3 g Sat Fat, 0 g Trans Fat, 49 mg Chol, 337 mg Sod, 19 g Carb, 1 g Fib, 27 g Prot, 20 mg Calc. **POINTS** value: **6.**

● ● ●

INDIVIDUAL MEAT LOAVES WITH PEPPERS & SUN-DRIED TOMATOES

prep 15 MIN   *cook* 20 MIN   *serves* 4

1   large red bell pepper, cut
    into thin strips

1   large onion, thinly sliced

⅓   cup thinly sliced dry-packed
    sun-dried tomatoes

2   teaspoons olive oil

½   teaspoon dried oregano

½   teaspoon salt

¼   teaspoon black pepper

1   pound ground lean beef
    (7% fat or less)

¼   cup Italian-seasoned dried
    bread crumbs

¼   cup + 2 tablespoons
    ketchup

1   large egg, lightly beaten

1   garlic clove, minced

¼   cup water

1 Preheat the grill to medium-high or prepare a medium-high fire using the direct method (see page 13). Tear off 4 (15 x 18-inch) sheets of heavy-duty foil and spray the centers with nonstick spray.

2 Combine the bell pepper, onion, sun-dried tomatoes, oil, oregano, ¼ teaspoon of the salt, and ⅛ teaspoon of the pepper in a medium bowl; set aside.

3 Put the beef, bread crumbs, ¼ cup of the ketchup, the egg, garlic, and the remaining ¼ teaspoon salt and ⅛ teaspoon pepper in a bowl; mix until combined. With damp hands, divide the mixture into 4 equal portions and shape each into a 2½ x 4½-inch loaf.

4 Place one-fourth of the bell pepper mixture on each foil sheet; drizzle with the water. Place 1 meat loaf on each portion of bell pepper mixture; top evenly with the remaining 2 tablespoons ketchup.

5 To close the packets, bring the two opposite long sides of the foil up to meet in the center; fold the edges over twice, making ½-inch-wide folds, to seal tightly. Double-fold the open sides, making ½-inch-wide folds, to seal tightly.

6 Place the packets on the grill rack and grill, covered, until an instant-read thermometer inserted into the center of a meat loaf registers 160°F, about 20 minutes. With a wide spatula, transfer the packets to a cutting board; carefully open, standing back to avoid the steam. Transfer the meat loaves and vegetables to each of 4 plates and drizzle with the juices.

PER SERVING (1 meat loaf and 1 cup vegetable mixture): 283 Cal, 11 g Fat, 4 g Sat Fat, 0 g Trans Fat, 117 mg Chol, 754 mg Sod, 20 g Carb, 3 g Fib, 26 g Prot, 54 mg Calc. **POINTS** value: **6.**

• • •

PORK TENDERLOIN WITH AUTUMN FRUIT

prep 15 MIN   *cook* 15 MIN   *serves* 4

1   apple, halved, cored, and thinly sliced

1   small onion, thinly sliced

½   cup pitted prunes, halved

¼   cup dried cranberries

2   tablespoons finely chopped fresh sage

2   teaspoons olive oil

½   teaspoon salt

¼   teaspoon black pepper

¼   cup apple or orange juice

1   (1-pound) pork tenderloin, trimmed and cut into 12 slices

1   garlic clove, minced

Fresh sage leaves (optional)

1 Preheat the grill to medium-high or prepare a medium-high fire using the direct method (see page 13). Tear off 4 (15 x 18-inch) sheets of heavy-duty foil and spray the centers with nonstick spray.

2 Combine the apple, onion, prunes, cranberries, 1 tablespoon of the sage, the oil, ¼ teaspoon of the salt, and ⅛ teaspoon of the pepper in a medium bowl. Place one-fourth of the mixture in the center of each foil sheet; drizzle evenly with the apple juice. Sprinkle the pork with the remaining 1 tablespoon sage, the garlic, and the remaining ¼ teaspoon salt and ⅛ teaspoon pepper. Place 3 slices of pork on each portion of the apple mixture.

3 To close the packets, bring the two opposite long sides of the foil up to meet in the center; fold the edges over twice, making ½-inch-wide folds, to seal tightly. Double-fold the open sides, making ½-inch-wide folds, to seal tightly.

4 Place the packets on the grill rack and grill, covered, until the pork is cooked through, about 15 minutes. With a wide spatula, transfer the packets to a cutting board; carefully open, standing back to avoid the steam. Transfer the pork and apple mixture to each of 4 plates and drizzle with the juices. Top each serving with a few sage leaves if using.

PER SERVING (3 slices pork and 1 cup apple mixture): 268 Cal, 7 g Fat, 2 g Sat Fat, 0 g Trans Fat, 67 mg Chol, 345 mg Sod, 28 g Carb, 3 g Fib, 25 g Prot, 26 mg Calc. **POINTS** value: **5.**

●●●

HOISIN PORK BURGERS WITH ASIAN-STYLE SALAD

prep 15 MIN   *cook* 15 MIN   *serves* 4

1   pound ground lean pork

¼   cup plain dried bread crumbs

¼   cup chopped scallions

¼   cup + 1 tablespoon hoisin sauce

2   tablespoons reduced-sodium soy sauce

1   tablespoon lime juice

1   tablespoon honey

¼   teaspoon Asian (dark) sesame oil

¼   teaspoon ground ginger

1   small head Boston lettuce, torn into bite-size pieces (4 cups)

1   cucumber, peeled and thinly sliced

1   cup cherry tomatoes, halved

4   radishes, thinly sliced

1 Preheat the grill to medium-high or prepare a medium-high fire using the direct method (see page 13). Tear off 1 (18 x 20-inch) sheet of heavy-duty foil and spray the center with nonstick spray.

2 Combine the pork, bread crumbs, scallions, ¼ cup of the hoisin sauce, and the soy sauce in a medium bowl, mixing just until well combined. With damp hands, shape the mixture into 4 equal patties. Place the patties in the center of the foil sheet.

3 To close the packet, bring the two opposite long sides of the foil up to meet in the center; fold the edges over twice, making ½-inch-wide folds, to seal tightly. Double-fold the open sides, making ½-inch-wide folds, to seal tightly.

4 Place the packet on the grill rack and grill, covered, until an instant-read thermometer inserted into the side of a burger registers 160°F, about 15 minutes.

5 Meanwhile, whisk together the the lime juice, honey, sesame oil, ginger, and the remaining 1 tablespoon hoisin sauce in a small bowl. Combine the remaining ingredients in a serving bowl. Drizzle the dressing over and toss to coat evenly.

6 With a wide spatula, transfer the packet to a cutting board; carefully open, standing back to avoid the steam. Transfer a burger to each of 4 plates. Serve with the salad.

PER SERVING (1 burger and 1½ cups salad): 309 Cal, 11 g Fat, 3 g Sat Fat, 0 g Trans Fat, 75 mg Chol, 692 mg Sod, 23 g Carb, 3 g Fib, 29 g Prot, 58 mg Calc. **POINTS** value: **6.**

· · ·

ROSEMARY CHICKEN WITH BUTTERNUT SQUASH & APPLES ☑

prep 15 MIN   *cook* 25 MIN   *serves* 4

1   (1¼-pound) butternut squash, peeled, halved, seeded, and cut into ½-inch pieces

1   small onion, chopped

1   Granny Smith apple, unpeeled, chopped

1   garlic clove, minced

4   teaspoons chopped fresh rosemary or 1½ teaspoons dried

1   teaspoon salt

½   teaspoon black pepper

4   (6-ounce) bone-in chicken breast halves, skin removed

EXPRESS LANE

To cut down on your preparation time, use a bag of precut butternut squash, available in the produce department of supermarkets.

1 Preheat the grill to medium-high or prepare a medium-high fire using the direct method (see page 13). Tear off 4 (15 x 18-inch) sheets of heavy-duty foil and spray the centers with nonstick spray.

2 Bring 1 inch of water to a boil in a medium saucepan set over medium-high heat. Place the squash and onion in a steamer basket and set in the saucepan. Cover and steam until the vegetables are slightly softened, about 2 minutes. Carefully remove the steamer basket from the saucepan and transfer the squash and onion to a large bowl. Add the apple, garlic, 2 teaspoons of the rosemary, ½ teaspoon of the salt, and ¼ teaspoon of the pepper; toss to combine.

3 Place one-fourth of the squash mixture in the middle of each foil sheet. Sprinkle the chicken evenly with the remaining 2 teaspoons rosemary, ½ teaspoon salt, and ¼ teaspoon pepper; place 1 chicken breast half on each portion of the squash mixture. To close the packets, bring the two opposite long sides of the foil up to meet in the center; fold the edges over twice, making ½-inch-wide folds, to seal tightly. Double-fold the open sides, making ½-inch-wide folds, to seal tightly.

4 Place the packets on the grill rack and grill, covered, until the chicken is cooked through, about 25 minutes. With a wide spatula, transfer the packets to a cutting board; carefully open, standing back to avoid the steam. Transfer the chicken and vegetables to each of 4 plates and drizzle with the juices.

PER SERVING (1 chicken breast half and generous 1 cup squash mixture): 218 Cal, 4 g Fat, 1 g Sat Fat, 0 g Trans Fat, 73 mg Chol, 661 mg Sod, 18 g Carb, 3 g Fib, 28 g Prot, 66 mg Calc. **POINTS** value: **4.**

CHICKEN WITH SPINACH
& TOMATOES

CHICKEN WITH SPINACH & TOMATOES ☑

prep 10 MIN   *cook* 20 MIN   *serves* 4

3 cups lightly packed baby spinach

2 large tomatoes, chopped

¼ cup pitted brine-cured kalamata olives, chopped

½ teaspoon dried oregano

4 (¼-pound) skinless boneless chicken breast halves

2 teaspoons grated lemon zest

½ teaspoon salt

¼ teaspoon black pepper

¼ cup crumbled fat-free feta cheese

GOOD IDEA

Complete the meal by serving with pasta. One cup cooked whole-wheat penne will increase the per-serving *POINTS* value by *3.*

1 Preheat the grill to medium-high or prepare a medium-high fire using the direct method (see page 13). Tear off 4 (15 x 18-inch) sheets of heavy-duty foil and spray the centers with nonstick spray.

2 Place one-fourth of the spinach in the middle of each foil sheet. Combine the tomatoes, olives, and ¼ teaspoon of the oregano in a medium bowl. Place one-fourth of the tomato mixture on each mound of spinach.

3 Sprinkle the chicken with the lemon zest, salt, pepper, and the remaining ¼ teaspoon oregano. Place 1 piece of chicken each mound of vegetables. To close the packets, bring the two opposite long sides of the foil up to meet in the center; fold the edges over twice, making ½-inch-wide folds, to seal tightly. Double fold the open sides, making ½-inch-wide folds to seal completely.

4 Place the packets on the grill rack and grill, covered, until the chicken is cooked through, about 20 minutes. With a wide spatula, transfer the packets to a cutting board; carefully open, standing back to avoid the steam. Transfer the chicken and vegetables to each of 4 plates. Drizzle with the juices and sprinkle evenly with the feta.

PER SERVING (1 chicken breast half and ¾ cup vegetable mixture): 192 Cal, 5 g Fat, 1 g Sat Fat, 0 g Trans Fat, 70 mg Chol, 459 mg Sod, 6 g Carb, 2 g Fib, 30 g Prot, 56 mg Calc. *POINTS* value: *4.*

• • •

GREEK-STYLE CHICKEN WITH CUCUMBER-YOGURT SAUCE ☑

prep 20 MIN *cook* 30 MIN *serves* 4

4 (¼-pound) red potatoes, scrubbed, halved, and thinly sliced

1 small red bell pepper, cut into thin strips

1 small onion, thinly sliced

1 pound chicken tenders

2 garlic cloves, minced

3 teaspoons olive oil

2 teaspoons grated lemon zest

½ teaspoon dried oregano

¼ + ⅛ teaspoon salt

5 tablespoons lemon juice

¾ cup plain fat-free yogurt

1 small cucumber, peeled, seeded, and grated

1 tablespoon chopped flat-leaf parsley

1 Spray a vegetable grill topper with olive oil nonstick spray and place on the grill rack. Preheat the grill to medium-high or prepare a medium-high fire using the direct method (see page 13). Tear off 4 (15 x 18-inch) sheets of heavy-duty foil and spray the centers with olive oil nonstick spray.

2 Combine the potatoes, bell pepper, and onion in a bowl; spray with nonstick spray. Spread on the grill topper and grill, turning, until almost tender, about 8 minutes; transfer to bowl. Add the chicken, half the garlic, 2 teaspoons of the oil, the lemon zest, oregano, and ¼ teaspoon of the salt to the bowl; toss.

3 Place one-fourth of the chicken mixture in the middle of each foil sheet; drizzle with 4 tablespoons of the lemon juice. To close the packets, bring the two opposite long sides of the foil up to meet in the center; fold the edges over twice, making ½-inch-wide folds, to seal tightly. Double-fold the open sides, making ½-inch-wide folds, to seal tightly.

4 Place the packets on the grill rack and grill, covered, until the chicken is cooked through, about 20 minutes.

5 Meanwhile, combine the yogurt, cucumber, parsley, and the remaining 1 tablespoon lemon juice, 1 teaspoon oil, garlic, and ⅛ teaspoon salt in a serving bowl.

6 With a wide spatula, transfer the packets to a cutting board; carefully open, standing back to avoid the steam. Transfer the chicken and vegetables to each of 4 plates and drizzle with the juices. Serve with the sauce.

GOOD IDEA

Serve the versatile cucumber-yogurt sauce as an accompaniment to grilled salmon, lamb, or beef. Refrigerated in a covered container, it will keep up to 4 days.

PER SERVING (¼ of chicken, generous 1 cup vegetables, and 3 tablespoons sauce): 305 Cal, 7 g Fat, 2 g Sat Fat, 0 g Trans Fat, 69 mg Chol, 332 mg Sod, 29 g Carb, 4 g Fib, 30 g Prot, 147 mg Calc. **POINTS** value: **6.**

TURKEY SAUSAGE WITH APPLES & CABBAGE

prep **15 MIN**   *cook* **30 MIN**   *serves* **4**

4   cups packed thinly sliced savoy or green cabbage

2   Granny Smith apples, unpeeled, halved, cored, and thinly sliced

1   small onion, thinly sliced

2   teaspoons olive oil

1   garlic clove, minced

¼   teaspoon caraway seeds

¼   teaspoon salt

⅛   teaspoon black pepper

1   pound Italian-style turkey sausage links, cut into 1-inch pieces

¼   cup unsweetened apple juice

2   cups hot cooked white rice

1 Preheat the grill to medium-high or prepare a medium-high fire using the direct method (see page 13). Tear off 4 (15 x 18-inch) sheets of heavy-duty foil and spray the centers with nonstick spray.

2 Toss together the cabbage, apples, onion, oil, garlic, caraway seeds, salt, and pepper in a large bowl until well mixed. Place one-fourth of the cabbage mixture in the middle of each foil sheet, then top with one-fourth of the sausages; drizzle evenly with the apple juice.

3 To close the packets, bring the two opposite long sides of the foil up to meet in the center; fold the edges over twice, making ½-inch-wide folds, to seal tightly. Double-fold the open sides, making ½-inch-wide folds, to seal tightly.

4 Place the packets on the grill rack and grill, covered, until the sausages are cooked through, about 20 minutes. With a wide spatula, transfer the packets to a cutting board. Carefully open, standing back to avoid the steam. Transfer the sausage and cabbage mixture to each of 4 plates and drizzle with the juices. Serve with the rice.

PER SERVING (¼ of sausages, ¾ cup cabbage mixture, and ½ cup rice): 416 Cal, 15 g Fat, 3 g Sat Fat, 0 g Trans Fat, 104 mg Chol, 1150 mg Sod, 40 g Carb, 5 g Fib, 31 g Prot, 69 mg Calc. **POINTS** value: **9.**

• • •

SALMON WITH TOMATO-OLIVE SAUCE ☑

prep 15 MIN   *cook* 15 MIN   *serves* 4

3 cups cherry tomatoes, halved

⅓ cup pitted brine-cured kalamata olives, chopped

2 garlic cloves, minced

2 teaspoons grated lemon zest

2 teaspoons olive oil

½ teaspoon salt

¼ teaspoon black pepper

4 (¼-pound) skinless salmon fillets

2 tablespoons chopped flat-leaf parsley

1 Preheat the grill to medium-high or prepare a medium-high fire using the direct method (see page 13). Tear off 4 (15 x 18-inch) sheets of heavy-duty foil and spray the centers with olive oil nonstick spray.

2 Toss together the cherry tomatoes, olives, garlic, lemon zest, oil, ¼ teaspoon of the salt, and ⅛ teaspoon of the pepper in a medium bowl. Place one-fourth of the tomato mixture in the middle of each foil sheet.

3 Sprinkle the salmon evenly with the remaining ¼ teaspoon salt and ⅛ teaspoon pepper. Place 1 fillet on each portion of vegetables. To close the packets, bring the two opposite long sides of the foil up to meet in the center; fold the edges over twice, making ½-inch-wide folds, to seal tightly. Double-fold the open sides, making ½-inch-wide folds, to seal tightly.

4 Place the packets on the grill rack and grill, covered, until the salmon is just opaque in the center, about 15 minutes. With a wide spatula, transfer the packets to a cutting board; carefully open, standing back to avoid the steam. Transfer the salmon and vegetables to each of 4 plates; drizzle with the juices and sprinkle evenly with the parsley.

PER SERVING (1 salmon fillet and ¾ cup vegetables): 223 Cal, 10 g Fat, 2 g Sat Fat, 0 g Trans Fat, 75 mg Chol, 476 mg Sod, 7 g Carb, 2 g Fib, 26 g Prot, 45 mg Calc. **POINTS** value: **5.**

**SALMON WITH
TOMATO-OLIVE SAUCE**

• • •

TUNA WITH LEMONY WHITE BEANS ☑

prep **10 MIN**   *cook* **12 MIN**   *serves* **4**

1   (15½-ounce) can cannellini (white kidney) beans, rinsed and drained

1   tomato, chopped

2   teaspoons olive oil

2   teaspoons grated lemon zest

2   garlic cloves, minced

¼   teaspoon salt

¼   teaspoon black pepper

2   tablespoons lemon juice

4   (6-ounce) tuna steaks, 1 inch thick

2   tablespoons chopped flat-leaf parsley

1 Preheat the grill to medium-high or prepare a medium-high fire using the direct method (see page 13). Tear off 4 (15 x 18-inch) sheets of heavy-duty foil and spray the centers with olive oil nonstick spray.

2 Toss together the beans, tomato, oil, lemon zest, half of the garlic, ⅛ teaspoon of the salt, and ⅛ teaspoon of the pepper in a medium bowl. Place one-fourth of the bean mixture in the center of each foil sheet and drizzle evenly with the lemon juice.

3 Sprinkle the tuna with the remaining garlic, ⅛ teaspoon salt, and ⅛ teaspoon pepper. Place 1 tuna steak on each portion of the bean mixture. To close the packets, bring the two opposite long sides of the foil up to meet in the center; fold the edges over twice, making ½-inch-wide folds, to seal tightly. Double-fold the open sides, making ½-inch-wide folds, to seal tightly.

4 Place the packets on the grill rack and grill, covered, until the tuna is slightly pink in the center, about 12 minutes. With a wide spatula, transfer the packets to a cutting board; carefully open, standing back to avoid the steam. Transfer the tuna and bean mixture to each of 4 plates; drizzle with the juices and sprinkle with the parsley.

PER SERVING (1 tuna steak and ¾ cup bean mixture): 323 Cal, 10 g Fat, 3 g Sat Fat, 0 g Trans Fat, 89 mg Chol, 455 mg Sod, 21 g Carb, 5 g Fib, 36 g Prot, 92 mg Calc. **POINTS** value: **6.**

TILAPIA WITH TOMATO-ORANGE SAUCE

prep 15 MIN   *cook* 15 MIN   *serves* 4

2 large plum tomatoes, each cut into 8 wedges

2 large navel oranges, peeled and cut into sections

2 teaspoons olive oil

¾ teaspoon ground cumin

⅛ teaspoon crushed red pepper

2 (½-pound) tilapia fillets, halved crosswise

½ teaspoon salt

¼ teaspoon black pepper

1 Preheat the grill to medium-high or prepare a medium-high fire using the direct method (see page 13). Tear off 4 (15 x 18-inch) sheets of heavy-duty foil and spray the centers with olive oil nonstick spray.

2 Combine the tomatoes, oranges, oil, ½ teaspoon of the cumin, and the crushed red pepper in a medium bowl. Place one-fourth of the orange mixture in the middle of each foil sheet.

3 Sprinkle the tilapia with the salt, black pepper, and the remaining ¼ teaspoon cumin. Place a piece of fish on each portion of the tomato mixture. To close the packets, bring the two opposite long sides of the foil up to meet in the center; fold the edges over twice, making ½-inch-wide folds, to seal tightly. Double-fold the open sides, making ½-inch-wide folds, to seal tightly.

4 Place the packets on the grill rack and grill, covered, until tilapia is just opaque in the center, about 15 minutes. With a wide spatula, transfer the packets to a cutting board; carefully open, standing back to avoid the steam. Transfer tilapia and vegetables to each of 4 plates and drizzle with the juices.

GOOD IDEA

We chose tilapia for this quick-cooking dish, but any thin fish fillets will work equally well. Try catfish, perch, pompano, or sea bass.

PER SERVING (½ tilapia fillet and generous 1 cup tomato mixture): 174 Cal, 4 g Fat, 1 g Sat Fat, 0 g Trans Fat, 60 mg Chol, 390 mg Sod, 12 g Carb, 3 g Fib, 23 g Prot, 61 mg Calc. **POINTS** value: **3.**

•••

LEMON SHRIMP WITH TOMATOES, GREEN BEANS & FETA

prep 10 MIN   *cook* 10 MIN   *serves* 4

2 large tomatoes, cut into ½-inch dice

½ pound slender green beans or haricots verts, trimmed and halved crosswise

2 garlic cloves, minced

2 teaspoons olive oil

½ teaspoon dried oregano

½ teaspoon salt

¼ teaspoon pepper

1 pound large shrimp, peeled and deveined, tails left on if desired

2 teaspoons grated lemon zest

¼ cup crumbled reduced-fat feta cheese

1 Preheat the grill to medium-high or prepare a medium-high fire using the direct method (see page 13). Tear off 4 (15 x 18-inch) sheets of heavy-duty foil and spray the centers with nonstick spray.

2 Combine the tomatoes, green beans, garlic, oil, oregano, ¼ teaspoon of the salt, and ⅛ teaspoon of the pepper in a large bowl. Combine the shrimp, lemon zest, and the remaining ¼ teaspoon salt and ⅛ teaspoon pepper in a medium bowl. Place one-fourth of the tomato mixture in the center of each foil sheet. Place one-fourth of the shrimp on top of each portion of the tomato mixture.

3 To close the packets, bring the two opposite long sides of the foil up to meet in the center; fold the edges over twice, making ½-inch-wide folds, to seal tightly. Double-fold the open sides, making ½-inch-wide folds, to seal tightly.

4 Place the packets on the grill rack and grill, covered, until shrimp are just opaque in the center, about 12 minutes. With a wide spatula, transfer the packets to a cutting board; carefully open, standing back to avoid the steam. Transfer shrimp and tomato mixture to each of 4 large shallow soup bowls. Drizzle with the juices and sprinkle evenly with the feta.

PER SERVING (about 4 shrimp, about 1½ cups tomato mixture, and 1 tablespoon feta): 127 Cal, 4 g Fat, 1 g Sat Fat, 0 g Trans Fat, 109 mg Chol, 518 mg Sod, 10 g Carb, 3 g Fib, 15 g Prot, 88 mg Calc. **POINTS** value: **2.**

• • •

MISO-MARINATED TEMPEH

prep 15 MIN   *cook* 10 MIN   *serves* 6

¼ cup white miso

¼ cup water

2 tablespoons unseasoned rice vinegar

1 tablespoon canola oil

2 teaspoons reduced-sodium soy sauce

1 teaspoon grated peeled fresh ginger

1 teaspoon sugar

2 (8-ounce) packages plain tempeh, cut into bite-size pieces

4 scallions, cut into 1-inch pieces

1 cup small broccoli florets

1 red bell pepper, cut into thin strips

1 yellow squash, halved lengthwise and sliced

3 cups hot cooked brown rice

1 Preheat the grill to medium-high or prepare a medium-high fire using the direct method (see page 13). Tear off 6 (15 x 18-inch) sheets of heavy-duty foil and spray the centers with nonstick spray.

2 To make the marinade, whisk together the miso, water, vinegar, oil, soy sauce, ginger, and sugar in a large bowl until blended. Transfer half of the mixture to a cup; set aside. Add the tempeh, scallions, broccoli, bell pepper, and squash to the miso mixture in the bowl; toss to coat evenly.

3 Place one-fourth of the tempeh mixture in the center of each foil sheet. To close the packets, bring the two opposite long sides of the foil up to meet in the center; fold the edges over twice, making ½-inch-wide folds, to seal tightly. Double-fold the open sides, making ½-inch-wide folds, to seal tightly.

4 Place the packets on the grill rack and grill, covered, until the vegetables are crisp-tender, about 12 minutes. With a wide spatula, transfer the packets to a cutting board; carefully open, standing back to avoid the steam. Transfer the tempeh-miso mixture to each of 6 large shallow soup bowls and spoon the rice alongside. Drizzle evenly with the reserved miso mixture.

PER SERVING (1½ cups tempeh-vegetable mixture and ½ cup rice): 320 Cal, 12 g Fat, 2 g Sat Fat, 0 g Trans Fat, 0 mg Chol, 775 mg Sod, 37 g Carb, 8 g Fib, 19 g Prot, 120 mg Calc. **POINTS** value: **7.**

MOROCCAN-SPICED
ZUCCHINI WITH MINT

MOROCCAN-SPICED ZUCCHINI WITH MINT ☑

prep 15 MIN   *cook* 15 MIN   *serves* 4

1   tablespoon olive oil

2   garlic cloves, minced

2   teaspoons minced peeled
      fresh ginger

½   teaspoon salt

½   teaspoon ground cumin

¼   teaspoon ground coriander

⅛   teaspoon ground turmeric

3   zucchini, halved lengthwise
      and thinly sliced

1   small onion, thinly sliced

1   tablespoon lemon juice

1   tablespoon chopped
      fresh mint

1 Preheat the grill to medium-high or prepare a medium-high fire using the direct method (see page 13). Tear off 1(15 x 18-inch) sheet of heavy-duty foil and spray the center with olive oil nonstick spray.

2 Combine the oil, garlic, ginger, salt, cumin, coriander, and turmeric in a large bowl. Add the zucchini and onion; toss to coat evenly.

3 Place the zucchini mixture in the middle of the foil sheet. To close the packet, bring the two opposite long sides of the foil up to meet in the center; fold the edges over twice, making ½-inch-wide folds, to seal tightly. Double-fold the open sides, making ½-inch-wide folds, to seal tightly.

4 Place the packet on the grill rack and grill, covered, until the zucchini is crisp-tender, about 12 minutes. With a wide spatula, transfer the packet to a cutting board; carefully open, standing back to avoid the steam. Spoon the vegetable mixture into a serving bowl; drizzle with the lemon juice and sprinkle with the mint.

HOW WE DID IT

To peel fresh ginger easily, scrape away the skin with the side of a teaspoon.

PER SERVING (¾ cup): 68 Cal, 4 g Fat, 1 g Sat Fat, 0 g Trans Fat, 0 mg Chol, 312 mg Sod, 8 g Carb, 2 g Fib, 2 g Prot, 34 mg Calc. **POINTS** value: **1**.

● ● ●

HERB-GRILLED CORN

prep 10 MIN   *cook* 15 MIN   *serves* 4

4   ears of corn, husks and silk removed

4   teaspoons unsalted butter, melted

½   teaspoon salt

16   fresh cilantro sprigs

16   fresh large basil leaves

4   fresh thyme or rosemary sprigs

8   teaspoons water

1 Preheat the grill to medium-high or prepare a medium-high fire using the direct method (see page 13). Tear off 4 (12 x 18-inch) sheets of heavy-duty foil and spray the centers with nonstick spray.

2 Brush the corn evenly with the butter and sprinkle with the salt; place 1 ear of corn in the middle of each foil sheet. Place 4 cilantro sprigs, 4 basil leaves, and 1 thyme sprig on top of each ear of corn; sprinkle evenly with the water. To close the packets, bring the two opposite long sides of the foil up to meet in the center; fold the edges over twice, making ½-inch-wide folds, to seal tightly. Double-fold the open sides, making ½-inch-wide folds, to seal tightly.

3 Place the packets on the grill rack and grill, covered, until the corn is tender, about 15 minutes. With a wide spatula, transfer the packets to a cutting board; carefully open, standing back to avoid the steam. Discard the herbs.

PER SERVING (1 ear of corn): 142 Cal, 5 g Fat, 3 g Sat Fat, 0 g Trans Fat, 10 mg Chol, 312 mg Sod, 25 g Carb, 4 g Fib, 3 g Prot, 3 mg Calc. **POINTS** value: **2.**

FARM-STAND SIDE DISHES

Chapter 5

• • •

ASPARAGUS WITH LEMON & HERBS ☑

prep 10 MIN   *cook* 5 MIN   *serves* 4

1   (1-pound) bunch asparagus, trimmed

3   teaspoons olive oil

½   teaspoon salt

1   teaspoon grated lemon zest

1   tablespoon lemon juice

1   tablespoon unseasoned rice vinegar

⅛   teaspoon black pepper

1   pint cherry tomatoes

2   tablespoons chopped fresh basil

1   tablespoon chopped fresh dill

HOW WE DID IT

If you don't have a vegetable grill topper, a heavy cookie cooling rack works equally well.

1 Place a vegetable grill topper on the grill rack and spray with olive oil nonstick spray. Preheat the grill to medium or prepare a medium fire using the direct method (see page 13). If using wooden skewers, soak them in water 30 minutes.

2 Meanwhile, combine the asparagus, 1 teaspoon of the oil, and ¼ teaspoon of the salt in a large zip-close plastic bag. Squeeze out the air and seal the bag; turn the bag to coat the asparagus. Set aside.

3 To make the dressing, whisk together the lemon zest and juice, vinegar, pepper, and the remaining 2 teaspoons oil and ¼ teaspoon salt in a small bowl.

4 Thread the cherry tomatoes on 4 skewers. Place the asparagus on the grill topper and grill, turning, until lightly browned and tender, 5–7 minutes. After 3 minutes of grilling time, place the tomato skewers on the grill rack and grill until the tomatoes are heated through and the skins blister, 1–2 minutes on each side.

5 Transfer the asparagus to a platter. Slide the tomatoes off the skewers and scatter on the aparagus. Re-whisk the dressing and spoon it over the asparagus and tomatoes. Sprinkle with the basil and dill.

PER SERVING (¼ of vegetable mixture): 61 Cal, 4 g Fat, 1 g Sat Fat, 0 g Trans Fat, 0 mg Chol, 302 mg Sod, 6 g Carb, 3 g Fib, 2 g Prot, 28 mg Calc. **POINTS** value: **1.**

CLOCKWISE FROM THE LEFT:
ASPARAGUS WITH LEMON & HERBS,
GRILLED VEGETABLE CAPONATA,
PAGE 161, AND PORTABELLOS
STUFFED WITH PANZANELLA SALAD,
PAGE 148

•••

MEXICAN GRILLED CORN

prep **15 MIN**   *cook* **10 MIN**   *serves* **4**

4   ears of corn, husks and silk removed

3   tablespoons fat-free mayonnaise

½   teaspoon smoked paprika

¼   teaspoon salt

1   ounce aged (firm) goat cheese, grated

1   lime, cut into wedges

1 Spray the grill rack with nonstick spray. Preheat the grill to medium-high or prepare a medium-high fire using the direct method (see page 13).

2 Place the corn on the grill rack and grill, turning occasionally, until browned in spots and tender, 10–12 minutes.

3 Meanwhile, combine the mayonnaise, paprika, and salt in a cup.

4 With tongs, transfer the corn to a cutting board. Lightly spread the mayonnaise mixture all over the corn; sprinkle with the cheese, pressing lightly so it adheres. Spray the corn with nonstick spray and return it to the grill rack. Grill until the corn is heated through, about 1 minute on each side. Serve with the lime wedges.

PER SERVING (1 ear of corn): 154 Cal, 4 g Fat, 2 g Sat Fat, 0 g Trans Fat, 9 mg Chol, 279 mg Sod, 29 g Carb, 5 g Fib, 6 g Prot, 72 mg Calc. **POINTS** value: **3.**

● ● ●

EGGPLANT PARMESAN STACKS

prep 35 MIN   *cook* 30 MIN   *serves* 4

½   cup fresh bread crumbs

1   garlic clove, crushed
    through a press

¼   cup grated Parmesan
    cheese

2   small eggplants (¾ pound
    each)

¼   teaspoon salt

2   tomatoes, ends trimmed,
    each cut into 8 slices

8   large fresh basil leaves

8   tablespoons shredded
    fat-free mozzarella cheese

1 Preheat the grill to medium-high or prepare a medium-high fire using the direct method (see page 13).

2 Spray a medium grill-safe skillet with nonstick spray. Place the skillet to one side of the grill and preheat 5 minutes. Add the bread crumbs to the skillet and cook, stirring frequently, until lightly toasted, 2–4 minutes. Add the garlic and cook, stirring constantly, until fragrant, about 1 minute. Transfer to a small bowl and let cool slightly. Stir in the Parmesan; set aside.

3 Trim both ends off the eggplants and cut each eggplant into 6 rounds, about ¾ inch thick. Spray the eggplant slices on one side with nonstick spray and sprinkle with the salt. Place, sprayed side down, on the grill rack and grill until lightly charred and tender, 4–6 minutes on each side. Transfer the eggplant to a plate.

4 Top 4 of the largest eggplant slices with 1 slice of tomato and 1 basil leaf. Sprinkle each with 2 tablespoons mozzarella and 1 tablespoon crumb mixture. Repeat layering once. Top each stack with 1 slice of eggplant and sprinkle with the remaining crumb mixture. Press down lightly to compact the stacks. Transfer the stacks to a grill-safe 13 x 9-inch baking pan.

5 Place the pan on the grill rack and grill, covered, until the stacks are heated through, the cheese is melted, and the crumbs are browned, about 10 minutes, rotating the pan from the front to the back of the grill after 5 minutes. Transfer the stacks to a platter; let stand about 1 minute before serving.

PER SERVING (1 eggplant stack): 130 Cal, 3 g Fat, 1 g Sat Fat, 0 g Trans Fat, 7 mg Chol, 470 mg Sod, 19 g Carb, 4 g Fib, 9 g Prot, 233 mg Calc. **POINTS** value: **2.**

●●●

JAPANESE-STYLE EGGPLANT

prep 15 MIN   *cook* 10 MIN   *serves* 4

3   tablespoons reduced-
    sodium soy sauce

1   tablespoon packed
    brown sugar

1   tablespoon minced peeled
    fresh ginger

1   tablespoon unseasoned
    rice vinegar

2   garlic cloves, crushed
    through a press

4   Japanese eggplants, halved
    lengthwise

3   scallions, trimmed

1   teaspoon Asian (dark)
    sesame oil

2   teaspoons sesame seeds,
    toasted

1 Whisk together the soy sauce, brown sugar, ginger, vinegar, and garlic in a small bowl, then pour into a 10 x 15-inch jelly-roll pan. With a small knife, score the cut side of the eggplant in a crisscross pattern, making the cuts about ¼ inch deep and being careful not to cut through to the skin. Place the eggplant, cut side down, in the soy sauce mixture. Marinate about 30 minutes at room temperature.

2 Meanwhile, spray the grill rack with nonstick spray. Preheat the grill to medium or prepare a medium fire using the direct method (see page 13).

3 Spray the cut side of the eggplant with nonstick spray and place, cut side up, on the grill rack. Transfer any remaining marinade to a cup; set aside. Grill the eggplant until lightly charred and softened, 4–5 minutes on each side. Place the scallions on the grill rack and grill until tender, about 2 minutes on each side.

4 Transfer the eggplant to a platter and drizzle with the reserved marinade. Slice the scallions and sprinkle over the eggplant; drizzle with the sesame oiland sprinkle with the sesame seeds. Serve hot or at room temperature.

PER SERVING (2 eggplant halves): 100 Cal, 3 g Fat, 0 g Sat Fat, 0 g Trans Fat, 0 mg Chol, 405 mg Sod, 18 g Carb, 4 g Fib, 2 g Prot, 26 mg Calc. **POINTS** value: **1.**

● ● ●

HONEY & BALSAMIC VINEGAR–GRILLED FENNEL

prep 10 MIN   *cook* 10 MIN   *serves* 4

3   large fennel bulbs, trimmed

2   tablespoons balsamic vinegar

1   tablespoon honey

1   garlic clove, crushed through a press

¼   teaspoon salt

⅛   teaspoon black pepper

1 Spray the grill rack with nonstick spray. Preheat the grill to medium or prepare a medium fire using the direct method (see page 13).

2 Meanwhile, cut the fennel bulb lengthwise into ½-inch slices; set aside. Stir together 1 tablespoon of the vinegar and the remaining ingredients in a cup.

3 Spray the fennel with nonstick spray. Place on the grill rack and grill until tender and lightly browned, 3–4 minutes on each side. Brush with all of the honey-vinegar mixture; grill 1 minute longer.

4 Transfer the fennel to a serving bowl and drizzle with the remaining 1 tablespoon vinegar. Serve hot, warm, or at room temperature.

TRY IT

For the most delicious flavor, buy the best balsamic vinegar your wallet will allow. Look for the word *tradizionale* on the label to ensure its authenticity.

PER SERVING (¼ of fennel): 78 Cal, 1 g Fat, 0 g Sat Fat, 0 g Trans Fat, 0 mg Chol, 239 mg Sod, 18 g Carb, 5 g Fib, 2 g Prot, 89 mg Calc. **POINTS** value: *1.*

**LEEKS WITH ORANGE-TOMATO
VINAIGRETTE**

●●●

LEEKS WITH ORANGE-TOMATO VINAIGRETTE ☑

prep 20 MIN   *cook* 15 MIN   *serves* 4

4   large leeks (white and light green parts only)

1   small navel orange

1   tablespoon olive oil

1   tablespoon unseasoned rice vinegar

½   teaspoon salt

¼   teaspoon black pepper

¼   cup brine-cured pimento-stuffed olives, chopped

1   large plum tomato, halved lengthwise

2   tablespoons chopped fresh basil

1 Trim the leeks, leaving the root end intact. Cut the leeks lengthwise in half and swish well in a large bowl of cool water to remove all the sandy dirt.

2 Fill a large skillet with 1 inch of water and insert a steamer basket. Add the leeks; cover and bring to a boil. Reduce the heat to medium and cook until the leeks are tender when pierced with a knife, about 8 minutes. Transfer the leeks to a platter; set aside.

3 Spray the grill rack with olive oil nonstick spray. Preheat the grill to medium or prepare a medium fire using the direct method (see page 13).

4 Meanwhile, grate 2 teaspoons zest from the orange. With a small knife, cut away the peel and white pith from the orange; coarsely chop the flesh. Combine the orange zest, oil, vinegar, ¼ teaspoon of the salt, and the pepper in a small bowl. Stir in the chopped orange and the olives; set aside.

5 Spray the cut sides of the leeks and the tomato with nonstick spray. Sprinkle the leeks with the remaining ¼ teaspoon salt. Place the leeks and tomato, cut side down, on the grill rack and grill until the leeks are nicely browned and the tomato is softened but still holds its shape, 3–4 minutes on each side.

6 Arrange the leeks, cut side up, on a platter. Coarsely chop the tomato. Add the tomato and basil to the orange mixture and stir gently to mix; spoon over the leeks. Serve at once or cover and refrigerate up to several hours.

PER SERVING (1 leek and ¼ cup vinaigrette): 123 Cal, 6 g Fat, 1 g Sat Fat, 0 g Trans Fat, 0 mg Chol, 457 mg Sod, 16 g Carb, 3 g Fib, 2 g Prot, 70 mg Calc. **POINTS** value: **2.**

• • •

PORTOBELLOS STUFFED WITH PANZANELLA SALAD

prep 15 MIN   *cook* 15 MIN   *serves* 6

6   medium portobello mushrooms, stems removed

6   tablespoons reduced-fat Italian salad dressing

2   tomatoes, cut into ½-inch dice

4   (½-inch) slices French bread

1   kirby cucumber, quartered lengthwise and sliced

¼   cup sliced fresh basil

2   tablespoons chopped red onion

¼   cup grated Romano cheese

1 Preheat the grill to medium or prepare a medium fire using the direct method (see page 13).

2 Meanwhile, brush the mushrooms with 3 tablespoons of the salad dressing; set aside. Toss together the tomatoes and the remaining 3 tablespoons salad dressing in a medium bowl; set aside.

3 Place the slices of bread on the grill rack and grill until nicely toasted, about 2 minutes on each side; transfer to a plate. Place the mushrooms, rounded side down, on the grill rack and grill until tender, 4–6 minutes on each side.

4 Cut the bread into ½-inch pieces. Add the cucumber, basil, and red onion to the tomato mixture; gently stir in the bread pieces. Place a mushroom, rounded side down, on each of 6 plates. Fill evenly with the tomato mixture and sprinkle with the Romano.

GOOD IDEA

If you can't find kirby cucumbers, use a regular cucumber instead. Peel it, cut it in half, and remove the seeds with the tip of a teaspoon.

PER SERVING (1 stuffed mushroom) 115 Cal, 5 g Fat, 1 g Sat Fat, 0 g Trans Fat, 5 mg Chol, 344 mg Sod, 14 g Carb, 2 g Fib, 6 g Prot, 74 mg Calc. **POINTS** value: **2.**

POLENTA WITH ROSEMARY-GARLIC MUSHROOMS

prep 15 MIN   *cook* 20 MIN   *serves* 6

1 pound mixed mushrooms, halved if large

1 tablespoon olive oil

1 tablespoon reduced-sodium soy sauce

1 tablespoon water

2 garlic cloves, crushed through a press

1 teaspoon chopped fresh rosemary

¼ teaspoon salt

⅛ teaspoon black pepper

1 (18-ounce) tube refrigerated polenta, cut into 12 slices

½ cup shredded part-skim smoked mozzarella cheese

2 tablespoons chopped fresh parsley

1 tablespoon grated Parmesan cheese

1 Spray the grill rack with nonstick spray. Preheat the grill to medium-high or prepare a medium-high fire using the direct method (see page 13).

2 Meanwhile, put the mushrooms in a large bowl. Whisk together the oil, soy sauce, water, garlic, rosemary, salt, and pepper in a small bowl; drizzle over the mushrooms, tossing to coat evenly.

3 Spray a large grill-safe skillet with nonstick spray. Place the skillet to one side of the grill rack and preheat 5 minutes. Add the mushrooms to the skillet and cook, stirring frequently, until tender and lightly browned, about 5 minutes.

4 Meanwhile, spray the polenta slices on both sides with nonstick spray. Place on the grill rack and grill until nicely marked, 4–5 minutes. With a wide spatula, turn the polenta and sprinkle with the mozzarella. Grill until the polenta is nicely marked and the cheese is melted, about 4 minutes. Transfer the polenta to a platter. Spoon the mushrooms over the polenta and sprinkle with the parsley and Parmesan.

PER SERVING (2 topped polenta slices): 130 Cal, 5 g Fat, 2 g Sat Fat, 0 g Trans Fat, 6 mg Chol, 462 mg Sod, 15 g Carb, 1 g Fib, 7 g Prot, 91 mg Calc. **POINTS** value: **3.**

• • •

SMOKY-SWEET CHIPOTLE ONIONS

prep **15 MIN**   *cook* **20 MIN**   *serves* **6**

¼ cup red-wine vinegar

3 tablespoons honey

½ teaspoon finely chopped chipotles en adobo

½ teaspoon salt

2 Vidalia onions, cut into ½-inch slices

2 red onions, cut into ½-inch slices

1 Spray the grill rack with nonstick spray. Preheat the grill to medium or prepare a medium fire using the direct method (see page 13).

2 Meanwhile, combine the vinegar, honey, chipotles en adobo, and ¼ teaspoon of the salt in a small saucepan; bring to a boil over high heat. Reduce the heat to medium and cook until reduced to ¼ cup, about 5 minutes. Transfer 1 tablespoon of the glaze to a cup.

3 Spray the onion slices on both sides with cooking spray and sprinkle with the remaining ¼ teaspoon salt. Place the onions on the grill rack and grill until just tender and lightly browned, 6–8 minutes on each side. Brush the onions with half of the glaze; grill 1 minute, then turn and brush with the remaining glaze. Grill 1 minute longer. Transfer the onions to a serving dish. Drizzle with the reserved glaze and toss to coat evenly.

PER SERVING (about ½ cup): 70 Cal, 1 g Fat, 0 g Sat Fat, 0 g Trans Fat, 0 mg Chol, 204 mg Sod, 16 g Carb, 1 g Fib, 1 g Prot, 18 mg Calc. **POINTS** value: **1.**

MARINATED GRILL-ROASTED PEPPERS

prep 15 MIN   *cook* 15 MIN   *serves* 4

4   large red or yellow bell
    peppers or a combination,
    each cut into 4 slabs

1   tablespoon olive oil

3   large garlic cloves, thinly
    sliced

¼   teaspoon crushed red
    pepper

2   tablespoons balsamic
    vinegar

8   pitted brine-cured kalamata
    olives, thinly sliced

1   tablespoon capers, drained
    and rinsed

¼   teaspoon salt

1   tablespoon chopped
    fresh oregano

1 Preheat the grill to medium or prepare a medium fire using the direct method (see page 13).

2 Place the peppers on the grill rack and grill until the peppers are softened and the skins are blackened, about 6 minutes on each side. Put the peppers in a large zip-close plastic bag and seal the bag; let steam 10 minutes.

3 Meanwhile, combine the oil, garlic, and crushed red pepper in a small skillet and set over low heat. Cook, stirring frequently, until the garlic softens and turns golden brown along the edges, about 5 minutes; remove the skillet from the heat.

4 When cool enough to handle, peel the peppers and pile them on a platter. Add the vinegar, olives, capers, and salt to the garlic oil, stirring to combine. Spoon over the peppers and sprinkle with the oregano. Let the peppers stand at least 15 minutes or up 1 hour to allow the flavors to develop.

PER SERVING (4 pieces of pepper): 70 Cal, 4 g Fat, 1 g Sat Fat, 0 g Trans Fat, 0 mg Chol, 278 mg Sod, 7 g Carb, 2 g Fib, 1 g Prot, 28 mg Calc. **POINTS** value: **1.**

• • •

GRILLED CHILES RELLENOS

prep 25 MIN   *cook* 20 MIN   *serves* 4

4 poblano peppers

3 ears of corn, husks and silk removed

½ cup shredded reduced-fat Monterey Jack cheese

3 tablespoons chopped fresh cilantro

¾ teaspoon ground cumin

¼ teaspoon salt

1 Preheat the grill to high or prepare a hot fire using the direct method (see page 13).

2 Place the poblano peppers and corn on the grill rack and grill, turning occasionally, until the pepper skins are charred and the corn is browned in spots, about 10 minutes. With tongs, transfer the peppers to a large zip-close plastic bag and seal the bag; let steam about 10 minutes. Transfer the corn to a plate. When cool enough to handle, with a long serrated knife, cut off the corn kernels and put in a medium bowl.

3 Carefully peel the peppers. Make a 2-inch-long lengthwise slit in each pepper. With your fingers, remove the seeds and ribs. Add the remaining ingredients to the corn and mix well. With a spoon, fill the peppers evenly with the corn mixture. Press the cut edges of each pepper together to enclose the filling; put the stuffed peppers on a plate.

4 Spray a disposable foil pan or double layer of heavy-duty foil large enough to hold the peppers with nonstick spray; place on the grill rack. Place the peppers in the pan and grill, covered, until heated through and the cheese is melted, about 10 minutes. Using a wide spatula, transfer the chiles rellenos to a platter.

PER SERVING (1 filled pepper): 139 Cal, 4 g Fat, 2 g Sat Fat, 0 g Trans Fat, 9 mg Chol, 283 mg Sod, 23 g Carb, 5 g Fib, 7 g Prot, 113 mg Calc. **POINTS** value: **2.**

GRILLED CHILES RELLENOS AND
CORNMEAL-CRUSTED CHICKEN WITH
CORN-TOMATO RAGOUT, PAGE 66

GRILLED SMASHED ROSEMARY POTATOES

prep 10 MIN   *cook* 30 MIN   *serves* 4

1¼ pounds baby Yukon Gold potatoes

4 teaspoons olive oil

1½ teaspoons chopped fresh rosemary

2 large garlic cloves, finely chopped

¾ teaspoon salt

¼ teaspoon black pepper

1 Put the potatoes in a medium saucepan and add enough cold water to cover. Bring to a boil over medium-high heat. Reduce the heat and cook just until the potatoes are tender, about 15 minutes; drain.

2 When the potatoes are cool enough to handle, with a wide spatula, gently press down on each potato until ¾ inch thick. (The skins will split but the potatoes will stay together.)

3 Meanwhile, place a vegetable grill topper on the grill and spray with olive oil nonstick spray. Preheat the grill to medium or prepare a medium fire using the direct method (see page 13).

4 Combine the remaining ingredients in a cup; set aside. Place the potatoes on the grill topper and grill until browned, about 5 minutes on each side. Pile the potatoes into a serving bowl and sprinkle with the rosemary mixture.

PER SERVING (scant 1 cup): 149 Cal, 5 g Fat, 1 g Sat Fat, 0 g Trans Fat, 0 mg Chol, 451 mg Sod, 26 g Carb, 3 g Fib, 2 g Prot, 34 mg Calc. **POINTS** value: **3.**

●●●

BABY POTATOES WITH LEMON-MINT GREMOLATA ☑

prep 15 MIN   *cook* 25 MIN   *serves* 4

1¼ pounds baby red potatoes, halved

½ teaspoon salt

2 tablespoons chopped fresh mint

1½ teaspoons grated lemon zest

1 garlic clove, minced

2 teaspoons olive oil

⅛ teaspoon black pepper

EXPRESS LANE

To cut down on your kitchen time, use store-bought precooked potatoes, available in the produce section of some supermarkets.

1 Place a vegetable grill topper on the grill and spray with olive oil nonstick spray. Preheat the grill to medium-high or prepare a medium-high fire using the direct method (see page 13).

2 Meanwhile, put the potatoes and ¼ teaspoon of the salt in a medium saucepan and add enough cold water to cover. Bring to a boil over high heat; reduce the heat to medium and cook just until almost tender, 8–10 minutes. Drain well.

3 To make the gremolata, combine the mint, lemon zest, and garlic in a cup; set aside. Combine the potatoes, oil, the remaining ¼ teaspoon salt, and the pepper in a large bowl, tossing to coat the potatoes.

4 Place the potatoes on the grill topper and grill until browned and tender, about 5 minutes on each side. Transfer the potatoes to a serving bowl and sprinkle with the gremolata.

PER SERVING (scant 1 cup): 129 Cal, 2 g Fat, 0 g Sat Fat, 0 g Trans Fat, 0 mg Chol, 304 mg Sod, 26 g Carb, 4 g Fib, 2 g Prot, 34 mg Calc. **POINTS** value: **2.**

•••

CHILI-GLAZED SWEET POTATOES

prep **10 MIN**   *cook* **45 MIN**   *serves* **4**

4   sweet potatoes (½ pound each), peeled and cut lengthwise into ½-inch slices

1½ tablespoons reduced-sodium soy sauce

¼   cup Thai sweet red chili sauce

1   lime, cut into wedges

1 Half-fill a large pot with water and bring to a boil over high heat; add the sweet potatoes. Reduce the heat and cook until the potatoes are tender but still firm in the center, about 5 minutes; drain.

2 Meanwhile, spray the grill rack with nonstick spray. Preheat the grill to medium or prepare a medium fire using the indirect method (see page 13).

3 Spray the potato slices on both sides with nonstick spray. Place on the heated portion of the grill rack and grill until lightly browned, about 3 minutes on each side. Move the potatoes to the cooler portion of the grill rack and brush with the soy sauce. Grill, turning occasionally and brushing with the soy sauce until tender, about 20 minutes. Brush the potatoes with the chili sauce. Grill, turning the potatoes and brushing with the remaining chili sauce, until glazed, about 5 minutes. Serve with the lime wedges.

PER SERVING (¼ of potatoes): 169 Cal, 0 g Fat, 0 g Sat Fat, 0 g Trans Fat, 0 mg Chol, 498 mg Sod, 39 g Carb, 6 g Fib, 3 g Prot, 58 mg Calc. **POINTS** value: **3.**

•••

SUMMER SQUASH WITH FRESH MINT & FETA ☑

prep 15 MIN   *cook* 10 MIN   *serves* 4

1   tablespoon + 1 teaspoon red-wine vinegar

1   tablespoon olive oil

½   teaspoon Dijon mustard

1   small garlic clove, crushed through a press

½   teaspoon salt

¼   teaspoon black pepper

2   large zucchini, cut lengthwise into ½-inch slices

2   large summer squash, cut lengthwise into ½-inch slices

¼   cup torn fresh mint

¼   cup crumbled fat-free feta cheese

1 Preheat the grill to medium or prepare a medium fire using the direct method (see page 13).

2 Meanwhile, whisk together the vinegar, oil, mustard, garlic, ¼ teaspoon of the salt, and ⅛ teaspoon of the pepper in a small bowl. Spray the zucchini and summer squash with olive oil nonstick spray; sprinkle with the remaining ¼ teaspoon salt and ⅛ teaspoon pepper.

3 Place the zucchini and squash on the grill rack and grill until tender and lightly browned, 4–5 minutes on each side. Transfer to a platter. Re-whisk the dressing and drizzle over the squash; sprinkle with the mint and feta. Serve hot or at room temperature.

PER SERVING (¼ of squash mixture): 115 Cal, 5 g Fat, 1 g Sat Fat, 0 g Trans Fat, 1 mg Chol, 331 mg Sod, 12 g Carb, 4 g Fib, 8 g Prot, 56 mg Calc. **POINTS** value: **2.**

TOMATOES STUFFED WITH BREAD CRUMBS & PARMESAN

prep 15 MIN   *cook* 10 MIN   *serves* 4

1   garlic clove

½   cup lightly packed fresh basil leaves

1   tablespoon fat-free mayonnaise

1   tablespoon water

1   teaspoon Dijon mustard

¼   teaspoon salt

⅛   teaspoon black pepper

½   cup fresh bread crumbs

4   large tomatoes (8 ounces each), halved crosswise and seeded

¼   cup grated Parmesan cheese

PLAY IT SAFE

When cooking in a skillet on the grill, place the skillet close to the front or to one side of the grill so you don't have to reach across the hot grill for the handle.

1 Spray the grill rack with nonstick spray. Preheat the grill to medium or prepare a medium fire using the direct method (see page 13).

2 Meanwhile, finely chop the garlic in a mini food processor. Add the basil and process until chopped. Add the mayonnaise, water, mustard, salt, and pepper; process until well blended, scraping down the side of the bowl. Transfer to a cup and set aside.

3 Spray a medium grill-safe skillet with nonstick spray. Place on the grill rack and preheat for 5 minutes. Add the bread crumbs to the skillet and cook, stirring frequently, until golden, 3–5 minutes. Scrape the crumbs into a small bowl.

4 Spray the cut sides of the tomatoes with nonstick spray. Place, cut side down, on the grill rack and grill until the tomatoes are lightly charred and softened but still hold their shape, about 3 minutes. Transfer, cut side up, to a disposable foil baking pan. Spread the mayonnaise mixture evenly on the tops of the tomatoes. Add the Parmesan to the bread crumbs and lightly toss to mix; sprinkle evenly on the tomatoes.

5 Return the tomatoes, crumbed side up, to the grill rack. Grill, covered, until heated through, about 3 minutes.

PER SERVING (2 tomato halves): 84 Cal, 3 g Fat, 1 g Sat Fat, 0 g Trans Fat, 5 mg Chol, 365 mg Sod, 12 g Carb, 3 g Fib, 5 g Prot, 122 mg Calc. **POINTS** value: **1.**

TOMATOES STUFFED
WITH BREAD CRUMBS
& PARMESAN

●●●

TANDOORI-STYLE VEGETABLE KEBABS ☑

prep 20 MIN   *cook* 10 MIN   *serves* 6

¾ cup plain fat-free Greek-style yogurt

2 tablespoons lemon juice

2 garlic cloves, minced

1½ teaspoons grated peeled fresh ginger

1½ teaspoons ground cumin

½ teaspoon ground coriander

½ teaspoon curry powder

½ teaspoon salt

⅛ teaspoon cayenne

1 zucchini, halved lengthwise and cut into 1-inch pieces

1 red bell pepper, cut into 1-inch pieces

1½ cups small cauliflower florets

1 red onion, cut into 12 wedges

1 tablespoon chopped fresh cilantro

1 tablespoon chopped fresh mint

1 Whisk together ½ cup of the yogurt, the lemon juice, garlic, ginger, cumin, coriander, curry powder, ¼ teaspoon of the salt, and the cayenne in a large bowl. Add the zucchini, bell pepper, cauliflower, and red onion; stir until coated evenly with the yogurt mixture. Let stand at least 30 minutes or up to 1 hour.

2 Spray the grill rack with olive oil nonstick spray. Preheat the grill to medium or prepare a medium fire using the direct method (see page 13). If using wooden skewers, soak them in water 30 minutes.

3 To make the yogurt sauce, combine the remaining ¼ cup yogurt, the cilantro, and mint in a small bowl; set aside.

4 Thread the vegetables alternately on 6 (10-inch) skewers. Spray with nonstick spray and sprinkle with the remaining ¼ teaspoon salt. Place the skewers on the grill rack and grill, turning, until the vegetables are lightly charred and tender, about 8 minutes. Serve with the yogurt sauce.

PER SERVING (1 kebab and 1 tablespoon sauce): 49 Cal, 0 g Fat, 0 g Sat Fat, 0 g Trans Fat, 1 mg Chol, 235 mg Sod, 9 g Carb, 2 g Fib, 3 g Prot, 88 mg Calc. **POINTS** value: **1.**

GRILLED VEGETABLE CAPONATA

prep 20 MIN   *cook* 20 MIN   *serves* 10

1   eggplant (about 1¼ pounds), peeled and cut into ½-inch slices

1   red bell pepper, cut into 4 slabs

1   onion, cut into ½-inch slices

1   zucchini, cut lengthwise into ½-inch slices

3   large plum tomatoes, halved lengthwise

5   large garlic cloves, peeled

½   pound red grapes on the stem

3   tablespoons balsamic vinegar

½   teaspoon salt

1   large celery stalk, coarsely chopped

¼   cup pitted brine-cured green and black olives, chopped

1   tablespoon capers, drained

1 Spray the grill rack with olive oil nonstick spray. Preheat the grill to medium-high or prepare a medium-high fire using the direct method (see page 13).

2 Put the eggplant, bell pepper, onion, zucchini, and tomatoes in a jelly-roll pan and spray with nonstick spray. Transfer the vegetables, in batches, to the grill rack and grill, turning, until lightly charred and tender, 4–8 minutes, returning the vegetables to the pan when they are done.

3 Wrap the garlic in a double layer of heavy-duty foil. Place the garlic packet and grapes on the grill rack and grill, turning once, until the garlic is soft and the grape skins blister, about 8 minutes.

4 When the pepper and tomatoes are cool enough to handle, remove the blackened skins. Coarsely chop all the vegetables and put in a large bowl. Remove the grapes from the stems and add the grapes to the bowl. Remove the garlic from the foil; place in a small bowl and mash with the vinegar and salt. Add the celery, garlic mixture, olives, and capers to the vegetables; gently toss to combine. Serve the caponata at room temperature or refrigerate in an airtight container up to 3 days.

PER SERVING (½ cup): 65 Cal, 2 g Fat, 0 g Sat Fat, 0 g Trans Fat, 0 mg Chol, 194 mg Sod, 13 g Carb, 3 g Fib, 1 g Prot, 22 mg Calc. **POINTS** value: **1.**

GRILLED TRI-COLOR SALAD

• • •

GRILLED TRI-COLOR SALAD

prep 20 MIN *cook* 15 MIN *serves* 6

2 garlic cloves, peeled

4 anchovies, rinsed

2 tablespoons fat-free mayonnaise

½ teaspoon grated lemon zest

2 tablespoons lemon juice

1 tablespoon extra-virgin olive oil

1 tablespoon water

1 teaspoon balsamic vinegar

½ teaspoon salt

¼ teaspoon black pepper

3 large Belgian endive, trimmed

1 head radicchio

6 cups lightly packed baby arugula

1 ounce Parmesan cheese, made into shavings with a vegetable peeler

1 Half-fill a small saucepan with water and bring to a boil over medium-high heat; add the garlic. Reduce the heat and cook until softened, about 4 minutes. Transfer the garlic to a cup and let cool.

2 Preheat the grill to medium or prepare a medium fire using the direct method (see page 13).

3 Meanwhile, to make the dressing, put the garlic, anchovies, mayonnaise, lemon zest and juice, oil, water, vinegar, ¼ teaspoon of the salt, and the pepper in a mini food processor; process until the garlic is finely chopped and the dressing is well blended.

4 Cut the endive lengthwise in half. Cut the radicchio in half through the root end; cut each half into 3 wedges. Lightly spray the cut sides of the endive and radicchio with nonstick spray and sprinkle with the remaining ¼ teaspoon salt.

5 Place the endive and radicchio on the grill rack and grill until the endive is lightly browned and tender, 3–4 minutes on each side and the radicchio is lightly browned, about 2 minutes on each side. Remove the core from the radicchio wedges. Cut the radicchio wedges and endive halves lengthwise in half; let cool.

6 Combine the endive, radicchio, arugula, and dressing in a large bowl; gently toss to coat evenly. Spoon the salad onto a platter and top with the Parmesan shavings.

GOOD IDEA

Blanching the garlic instead of using it raw gives the dressing a mellow garlic flavor. When prepping the endive, trim a thin slice off the root end.

PER SERVING (generous 1 cup): 76 Cal, 4 g Fat, 1 g Sat Fat, 0 g Trans Fat, 6 mg Chol, 441 mg Sod, 6 g Carb, 3 g Fib, 5 g Prot, 143 mg Calc. **POINTS** value: **1.**

• • •

GRILL-ROASTED FALL VEGETABLES ☑

prep 20 MIN   *cook* 35 MIN   *serves* 4

1   butternut squash (1¾ pounds), peeled, seeded, and cut into 1-inch chunks

¼   cup water

1   (10-ounce) container Brussels sprouts, halved

1   gala or Golden Delicious apple, unpeeled, cut into 8 wedges and cored

6   small shallots, halved lengthwise

4   garlic cloves, thinly sliced

2   teaspoons olive oil

2   teaspoons chopped fresh thyme or ¾ teaspoon dried

8   fresh sage leaves

¼   teaspoon salt

¼   teaspoon black pepper

2   tablespoons balsamic vinegar

1 Preheat the grill to medium-high or prepare a medium-high fire using the indirect method (see page 13). Spray a vegetable grill topper with olive oil nonstick spray and place the topper on the heated portion of the grill to preheat.

2 Combine the squash and water in a medium microwavable bowl. Cover with plastic wrap, turning back one corner; microwave on High just until the squash is tender when pierced with a knife, about 4 minutes, stirring after 2 minutes.

3 Spread the Brussels sprouts, apple, and shallots on the grill topper. Grill, covered, until the vegetables are well-marked, about 2 minutes on each side.

4 Spray a jelly-roll pan or large disposable foil pan with nonstick spray. Transfer the vegetables to the pan. Add the squash and any remaining water, the garlic, oil, thyme, sage, salt, and pepper; tossing to mix well. Spread the vegetables in an even layer.

5 Place the pan on the cooler portion of the grill rack and grill, covered, stirring, until the vegetable are tender, 25–30 minutes. Transfer the vegetable mixture to a serving bowl and stir in the vinegar.

EXPRESS LANE

To save time, pick up precut butternut squash in the produce section of your supermarket. You will need about 1¼ pounds squash.

PER SERVING (generous 1 cup): 168 Cal, 3 g Fat, 0 g Sat Fat, 0 g Trans Fat, 0 mg Chol, 176 mg Sod, 36 g Carb, 6 g Fib, 5 g Prot, 124 mg Calc. **POINTS** value: **3.**

THE GOODNESS
OF GRAINS

Chapter 6

• • •

PIZZA MARGHERITA

prep 50 MIN   *cook* 10 MIN   *serves* 6

PIZZA DOUGH

1½ cups warm water
(105°–115°F)

2   teaspoons olive oil

1   (¼-ounce) package active
dry yeast

1   teaspoon sugar

4   cups all-purpose flour

⅔   cup whole-wheat flour

¼   teaspoon salt

TOPPING

4   large plum tomatoes,
seeded and coarsely
chopped

1   tablespoon olive oil

¼   teaspoon salt

¾   cup shredded part-skim
mozzarella cheese

3   tablespoons grated
Parmesan cheese

1   cup lightly packed fresh
basil leaves

1 To make the dough, stir together the water, oil, yeast, and sugar in a small bowl. Let stand until bubbly, about 5 minutes. Combine the flours and salt in a food processor; pulse until combined. With the machine running, pour the yeast mixture through the feed tube; process until a soft dough forms, about 2 minutes.

2 Turn the dough onto a lightly floured surface and knead until smooth. Spray a large bowl with nonstick spray; add the dough and turn to coat. Cover with plastic wrap and let rise in a warm place until doubled in volume, 2–3 hours.

3 Meanwhile, generously spray the grill rack with nonstick spray and preheat the grill to high or prepare a hot fire using the direct method (see page 13). Lightly flour 2 baking sheets.

4 Divide the dough into 6 equal pieces and shape into balls. Roll 1 piece of dough into an 8-inch round; place on a baking sheet. Repeat.

5 Place 1 dough round on the grill rack and grill until browned on the bottom, about 1 minute. Turn the dough and grill just until the bottom stiffens but is not colored, about 30 seconds. Return the crust to the baking sheet, browned side up, and repeat with the remaining dough rounds. Combine the tomatoes, oil, and salt in a bowl. Sprinkle the tomatoes evenly over the crusts. Sprinkle with the mozzarella and Parmesan and top with the basil. Grill the pizzas, covered, in batches if necessary, until the cheese melts, 2–3 minutes.

PER SERVING (1 pizza): 453 Cal, 9 g Fat, 3 g Sat Fat, 0 g Trans Fat, 10 mg Chol, 334 mg Sod, 77 g Carb, 5 g Fib, 16 g Prot, 179 mg Calc. **POINTS** value: **9.**

PIZZA MARGHERITA

• • •

RED ONION & GOAT CHEESE PIZZA

prep **20 MIN**   *cook* **20 MIN**   *serves* **4**

2   small red onions, halved through the root end

1   (12-inch) prebaked pizza crust

⅓   cup barbecue sauce

2   ounces soft (mild) goat cheese, crumbled

1   teaspoon fresh thyme leaves

Pinch black pepper

1 Spray the grill rack with nonstick spray and preheat the grill to medium-high or prepare a medium-high fire using the direct method (see page 13).

2 Place the red onions on the grill rack and grill until browned and beginning to soften, about 15 minutes; transfer to a cutting board. When cool enough to handle, cut the onions into ¼-inch slices. Set aside.

3 Place the pizza crust, top side down, on the grill rack and grill until heated through, 3–5 minutes. With tongs, turn the crust over and spread with the barbecue sauce. Sprinkle evenly with the onions, goat cheese, thyme, and pepper. Return to the grill rack and grill, covered, until the cheese is softened, about 3 minutes. With tongs, grab an edge of the pizza and slide it onto a cutting board. Cut into 4 equal wedges.

PER SERVING (1 wedge): 263 Cal, 7 g Fat, 3 g Sat Fat, 0 g Trans Fat, 7 mg Chol, 568 mg Sod, 43 g Carb, 2 g Fib, 7 g Prot, 47 mg Calc. **POINTS** value: **5.**

●●●

GRILLED SAUSAGE & PEPPER HEROES

prep 25 MIN   *cook* 20 MIN   *serves* 4

10   ounces hot or sweet Italian-style turkey sausage links

2   small orange or red bell peppers

2   small red onions, halved through the root end

1   cup packed baby spinach (2 ounces), washed and spun dry

3   tablespoons finely chopped fresh parsley

1   tablespoon balsamic vinegar

¼   teaspoon black pepper

4   (8-inch) whole-wheat hero rolls

GOOD IDEA

For extra crunch, place the rolls on the grill and lightly toast.

1 Spray the grill rack with nonstick spray and preheat the grill to medium-high or prepare a medium-high fire using the direct method (see page 13).

2 Place the sausages, bell peppers, and red onions on the grill rack and grill, turning, until the sausages are cooked through, the peppers are blackened on all sides, and the onions are browned and beginning to soften, 15–20 minutes.

3 Put the peppers in a large zip-close plastic bag and let steam 10 minutes.

4 When cool enough to handle, peel the peppers and remove the seeds, then cut into ½-inch strips. Transfer to a large bowl. When cool enough to handle, cut the sausages on the diagonal into ½-inch slices. Add to the peppers in the bowl. Cut the onions into ¼-inch slices and add to the bowl. Add the spinach, parsley, vinegar, and black pepper; toss to mix well.

5 Split the rolls without cutting all the way through. With your fingers, remove a bit of the bready centers; discard. Fill the rolls evenly with the sausage and pepper mixture.

PER SERVING (1 sandwich): 256 Cal, 9 g Fat, 2 g Sat Fat, 0 g Trans Fat, 65 mg Chol, 671 mg Sod, 23 g Carb, 4 g Fib, 21 g Prot, 65 mg Calc. **POINTS** value: **5.**

• • •

SHRIMP & ARUGULA PANINI

prep **30 MIN**   *cook* **10 MIN**   *serves* **4**

1   pound large shrimp, peeled and deveined

8   fresh basil leaves, thinly sliced

1   tablespoon extra-virgin olive oil

¼   teaspoon salt

⅛   teaspoon black pepper

8   slices whole-grain country-style bread

1   (4.4-ounce) package light garlic and herb cheese spread

20 arugula leaves

2   tomatoes, each cut into 4 thick slices

1 Spray the grill rack with nonstick spray and preheat the grill to medium or prepare a medium fire using the direct method (see page 13). Soak 5 (12-inch) wooden skewers in water 30 minutes.

2 Meanwhile, toss together the shrimp, basil, oil, salt, and pepper in a large bowl; refrigerate about 20 minutes. Thread about 4 shrimp on each skewer.

3 Place the shrimp and slices of bread on the grill rack and grill, turning, until the shrimp are just opaque throughout and the bread is golden brown and nicely marked, 3–5 minutes.

4 Spread the cheese evenly on one side of each slice of bread. Evenly layer the arugula, tomato slices, and shrimp on 4 slices of the bread. Top with the remaining slices of bread and cut the sandwiches in half.

PER SERVING (1 sandwich): 320 Cal, 13 g Fat, 6 g Sat Fat, 0 g Trans Fat, 134 mg Chol, 767 mg Sod, 30 g Carb, 5 g Fib, 22 g Prot, 240 mg Calc. **POINTS** value**: 7.**

● ● ●

LEMONY COUSCOUS & GRILLED VEGETABLE SALAD ☑

prep **30 MIN** *cook* **20 MIN** *serves* **6**

2 (5-ounce) zucchini, ends trimmed and each cut lengthwise into 6 slices

1 large red bell pepper

1 small yellow bell pepper

1 small red onion, halved through the root end

1 cup whole-wheat couscous

¼ cup lemon juice

2 tablespoons chopped flat-leaf parsley

2 tablespoons chopped fresh dill

1 tablespoon olive oil

1½ teaspoons grated lemon zest

¼ teaspoon salt

¼ teaspoon black pepper

1 Spray the grill rack with olive oil nonstick spray and preheat the grill to medium-high or prepare a medium-high fire using the direct method (see page 13).

2 Place the zucchini, bell peppers, and red onion on the grill rack and grill, turning, until the zucchini and onion are browned and beginning to soften and the peppers are blackened on all sides, about 15 minutes.

3 Transfer the peppers to a large zip-close plastic bag and seal the bag; let steam 10 minutes.

4 When cool enough to handle, peel the peppers and remove the seeds. Cut into ½-inch pieces and put in a large bowl. Cut the zucchini into ½-inch pieces; add to the peppers in the bowl. Cut the onion into ¼-inch slices and add to the bowl; set aside.

5 Cook the couscous according to the package directions; add to the vegetables. Add the remaining ingredients and toss to mix well. Serve warm or at room temperature.

PER SERVING (about ¾ cup): 115 Cal, 3 g Fat, 0 g Sat Fat, 0 g Trans Fat, 0 mg Chol, 108 mg Sod, 21 g Carb, 4 g Fib, 4 g Prot, 29 mg Calc. **POINTS** value: **2.**

CHICKEN SOUVLAKI
SANDWICHES

• • •

CHICKEN SOUVLAKI SANDWICHES

prep 35 MIN   *cook* 15 MIN   *serves* 4

2 tablespoons finely chopped fresh mint

1 teaspoon olive oil

1 tablespoon red-wine vinegar

1 teaspoon fresh thyme leaves

¼ teaspoon salt

¼ teaspoon black pepper

4 (¼-pound) skinless boneless chicken breast halves

1 small garlic clove, chopped

1 cup plain fat-free yogurt

1 unpeeled kirby cucumber, cut into ¼-inch dice

4 (6-inch) pita breads

2 cups lightly packed thinly sliced romaine lettuce

½ small red onion, thinly sliced

2 tomatoes, each cut into 8 wedges

1 Combine 1 tablespoon of the mint, the oil, vinegar, thyme, ⅛ teaspoon of the salt, and ⅛ teaspoon of the pepper in a large zip-close plastic bag; add the chicken. Squeeze out the air and seal the bag; turn to coat the chicken. Refrigerate, turning the bag occasionally, at least 2 hours or up to 4 hours.

2 Meanwhile, spray the grill rack with nonstick spray. Preheat the grill to medium or prepare a medium fire using the direct method (see page 13).

3 With the side of a large knife, mash the garlic with the remaining ⅛ teaspoon salt until it forms a paste. Stir together the yogurt, cucumber, garlic paste, and the remaining 1 tablespoon mint, and ⅛ teaspoon pepper in a medium bowl; set aside.

4 Place the chicken on the grill rack and grill, turning, until cooked through, 10–12 minutes. When cool enough to handle, cut on the diagonal into ½-inch strips.

5 Cut each pita in half. Stuff each half with ¼ cup of the lettuce, one-eighth of the chicken, one-eighth of the onion, and 2 tomato wedges. Top each sandwich half with 2 tablespoons of the yogurt mixture.

FOOD NOTE

The Greek yogurt and cucumber sauce for these super tasty sandwiches is known as tzatziki (dzah-DZEE-kee).

PER SERVING (1 sandwich): 397 Cal, 8 g Fat, 2 g Sat Fat, 0 g Trans Fat, 74 mg Chol, 587 mg Sod, 42 g Carb, 3 g Fib, 36 g Prot, 207 mg Calc. **POINTS** value: **8.**

CHICKEN & WILD RICE SALAD WITH CRANBERRIES & PECANS

prep **35 MIN** *cook* **50 MIN** *serves* **4**

1   cup brown and wild rice blend

¼   teaspoon salt

1   cup sugar snap peas, trimmed

1   skinless boneless chicken breast half

2   scallions, thinly sliced

⅓   cup dried cranberries

⅓   cup pecans, toasted

6   tablespoons orange juice

2   tablespoons honey

1   tablespoon olive oil

¼   teaspoon black pepper

1   (8¼-ounce) can mandarin oranges in light syrup, drained

1 Cook the rice according to the package directions, using ⅛ teaspoon of the salt and no butter, scattering the sugar snap peas on top of the rice for the last 5 minutes of standing time.

2 Meanwhile, spray the grill rack with nonstick spray and preheat the grill to medium or prepare a medium fire using the direct method (see page 13).

3 Place the chicken on the grill rack and grill, turning, until cooked through, 10–12 minutes. Transfer to a cutting board. When cool enough to handle, tear into ½-inch pieces.

4 Transfer the rice and peas to a serving bowl. Add the chicken and all of the remaining ingredients except the oranges; toss until well combined. Gently stir in the oranges.

PER SERVING (1½ cups): 406 Cal, 11 g Fat, 1 g Sat Fat, 0 g Trans Fat, 18 mg Chol, 494 mg Sod, 66 g Carb, 6 g Fib, 14 g Prot, 38 mg Calc. **POINTS** value: **8**.

• • •

BROWN RICE SALAD WITH SHIITAKE MUSHROOMS & ORANGES ✓

prep 35 MIN   *cook* 50 MIN   *serves* 6

1   cup brown rice

¼   teaspoon + pinch salt

1   small red bell pepper

10 ounces fresh shiitake
    mushrooms, stems removed

⅓   cup chopped fresh parsley

1   tablespoon extra-virgin
    olive oil

1   tablespoon lemon juice

⅛   teaspoon black pepper

2   navel oranges, peeled and
    cut into ½-inch pieces

1   red onion, thinly sliced

1 Cook the brown rice according to the package directions using the pinch of salt and no butter.

2 Meanwhile, spray the grill rack with olive oil nonstick spray and preheat the grill to medium-high or prepare a medium-high fire using the direct method (see page 13).

3 Place the bell pepper and mushrooms on the grill rack and grill, turning, until the pepper is blackened on all sides, about 15 minutes and the mushrooms are softened, browned, and nicely marked, 8–10 minutes. Transfer the pepper to a large zip-close plastic bag and seal the bag; let steam 10 minutes.

4 When cool enough to handle, peel the pepper and remove the seeds; cut into ½-inch pieces. Cut the mushrooms into ¼-inch slices.

5 To make the dressing, whisk together the parsley, oil, lemon juice, the remaining ¼ teaspoon salt, and the black pepper in a serving bowl. Add the brown rice, bell pepper, mushrooms, oranges, and red onion; toss until well combined.

FOOD NOTE

Shiitake mushrooms have stems that are too tough to eat even after they are cooked. Remove them by snipping them off close to the caps.

PER SERVING (1 cup): 178 Cal, 3 g Fat, 1 g Sat Fat, 0 g Trans Fat, 0 mg Chol, 129 mg Sod, 33 g Carb, 6 g Fib, 5 g Prot, 40 mg Calc. **POINTS** value: **3.**

• • •

SPAGHETTI WITH SHRIMP, TOMATOES & PEAS

prep **25 MIN**   *cook* **15 MIN**   *serves* **4**

6   ounces whole-wheat spaghetti

1   (10-ounce) package frozen peas, thawed

1   pint red or yellow grape tomatoes, halved

½   cup chopped flat-leaf parsley

⅓   cup chopped fresh basil

1   tablespoon extra-virgin olive oil

¼   teaspoon salt

¼   teaspoon black pepper

1   pound large shrimp, peeled and deveined

1 Spray the grill rack with olive oil nonstick spray and preheat the grill to medium or prepare a medium fire using the direct method (see page 13). Soak 5 (12-inch) wooden skewers in water 30 minutes.

2 Meanwhile, cook the spaghetti according to the package directions, omitting the salt and adding the peas for the last 1 minute of cooking time. Drain in a colander, then rinse under cold running water; drain again. Transfer the spaghetti and peas to a large bowl. Add the tomatoes, parsley, basil, oil, salt, and pepper; toss until well combined. Set aside.

3 Thread about 4 shrimp on each skewer. Place the shrimp on the grill rack and grill, turning, until just opaque throughout, about 5 minutes. Slide the shrimp off the skewers and add to the pasta mixture. Toss until well combined, then divide evenly among 4 large bowls.

PER SERVING (about 1¼ cups): 291 Cal, 5 g Fat, 1 g Sat Fat, 0 g Trans Fat, 107 mg Chol, 327 mg Sod, 43 g Carb, 7 g Fib, 22 g Prot, 79 mg Calc. ***POINTS*** value: **5.**

SPAGHETTI WITH SHRIMP,
TOMATOES & PEAS

• • •

QUINOA WITH GRILLED TEMPEH & VEGETABLES ☑

prep 25 MIN   *cook* 15 MIN   *serves* 4

2   zucchini, ends trimmed and each cut lengthwise into 6 slices

1   small red onion, halved through the root end

1   (8-ounce) package plain tempeh

¾   cup plain fat-free yogurt

1   tomato, seeded and chopped

¼   teaspoon curry powder

¼   teaspoon salt

Pinch cayenne

1   cup quinoa

Fresh cilantro leaves

1 Spray the grill rack with olive oil nonstick spray and preheat the grill to medium-high or prepare a medium-high fire using the direct method (see page 13).

2 Place the zucchini, red onion, and tempeh on the grill rack and grill, turning, until the zucchini and onion are browned and beginning to soften and the tempeh is heated through, 10–15 minutes.

3 When cool enough to handle, cut the zucchini into ½-inch pieces and transfer to a large bowl. Cut the onion into ¼-inch slices and add to the bowl. Cut the tempeh crosswise into ½-inch slices, then cut across to make ½-inch pieces; set aside.

4 To make the dressing, stir together the yogurt, tomato, curry powder, ⅛ teaspoon of the salt, and the cayenne in a medium bowl; set aside.

5 Cook the quinoa according to the package directions. Add the quinoa and the remaining ⅛ teaspoon salt to the zucchini mixture in the bowl; toss to combine well. Add the tempeh to the yogurt mixture and stir to coat evenly. Spoon about 1 cup of the quinoa mixture on each of 4 plates. Top evenly with the tempeh mixture and sprinkle with cilantro.

PER SERVING (1¼ cups): 323 Cal, 9 g Fat, 2 g Sat Fat, 0 g Trans Fat, 1 mg Chol, 209 mg Sod, 45 g Carb, 6 g Fib, 20 g Prot, 202 mg Calc. **POINTS** value: **6.**

SAUCES, SALSAS, RUBS & MARINADES

Chapter 7

●●●

CLASSIC AMERICAN BARBECUE SAUCE

prep **30 MIN**   *cook* **40 MIN**   *serves* **8**

1   tablespoon canola oil

1   small onion, finely chopped

1   garlic clove, finely chopped

1   cup water

1   cup ketchup

1   small red bell pepper, finely chopped

½   cup finely chopped celery with leaves

3   tablespoons packed brown sugar

2   tablespoons apple-cider vinegar

1   teaspoon Worcestershire sauce

¼   teaspoon salt

¼   teaspoon black pepper

3   tablespoons lemon juice

1 Heat the oil in a medium saucepan over medium heat. Add the onion and garlic; cook, stirring, until the onion begins to soften, about 5 minutes. Stir in all of the remaining ingredients except the lemon juice. Increase the heat to medium-high and bring to a boil. Reduce the heat and simmer, stirring occasionally, about 30 minutes. Remove the saucepan from the heat and let cool 5 minutes.

2 Transfer the sauce mixture, in batches if necessary, to a blender and puree. Stir in the lemon juice. Use at once or refrigerate in a covered container up to 1 week. Makes 2 cups.

PER SERVING (¼ cup): 37 Cal, 1 g Fat, 0 g Sat Fat, 0 g Trans Fat, 0 mg Chol, 212 mg Sod, 7 g Carb, 0 g Fib, 0 g Prot, 9 mg Calc. **POINTS** value: **1.**

• • •

LIME-AVOCADO SAUCE ☑

prep 15 MIN *cook* NONE *serves* 10

1 large shallot, minced (about ¼ cup)

½ teaspoon grated lime zest

2 tablespoons lime juice

¼ teaspoon salt

Pinch cayenne

2 ripe Hass avocados

¼ cup reduced-sodium chicken broth or water

1 Combine the shallot, lime zest and juice, salt, and cayenne in a food processor; pulse until well combined. Set aside.

2 Cut the avocados in half and remove the seeds. With a large spoon, scoop out the flesh. Add to the lime mixture and process until smooth. Add the chicken broth and process until well combined. Serve at once or press a piece of plastic wrap directly onto the surface and refrigerate up to 2 hours. Makes 1 cup.

PER SERVING (about 1½ tablespoons): 62 Cal, 5 g Fat, 1 g Sat Fat, 0 g Trans Fat, 0 mg Chol, 77 mg Sod, 4 g Carb, 2 g Fib, 1 g Prot, 7 mg Calc. ***POINTS*** value: *1.*

• • •

EGGPLANT–BELL PEPPER SPREAD ☑

prep 15 MIN   *cook* 25 MIN   *serves* 6

1   small eggplant (about ¾ pound)
2   red bell peppers
1   garlic clove, chopped
¼   teaspoon salt
2   pickled jalapeño peppers, seeded and minced
2   tablespoons red-wine vinegar
1   tablespoon canola oil
Pinch black pepper

FOOD NOTE

Ajvar (EYE-vahr) is the Serbian name for this tasty condiment, which is traditionally enjoyed with meats, cheeses, raw vegetables, and fish.

1 Spray the grill rack with olive oil nonstick spray. Preheat the grill to medium-high or prepare a medium-high fire using the direct method (see page 13).

2 With a fork, prick the eggplant in 4 places. Place the eggplant and bell peppers on the grill rack and grill, turning, until blackened on all sides, about 15 minutes. Put the eggplant on a cutting board. Transfer the bell peppers to a zip-close plastic bag and seal the bag; let steam 10 minutes. When the eggplant is cool enough to handle, peel off the skin and coarsely chop the flesh. Peel the bell peppers and remove the seeds; coarsely chop the flesh.

3 With the side of a large knife, mash the garlic and salt until it forms a paste.

4 Put the eggplant, bell peppers, garlic paste, and the remaining ingredients in a food processor and process until finely chopped.

5 Transfer the eggplant mixture to a medium nonstick skillet and set over medium heat. Cook, stirring, until most of the liquid is evaporated, about 10 minutes. Remove the skillet from the heat and let cool to room temperature. Serve at once or refrigerate in a covered container up to 1 week. Makes 1½ cups.

PER SERVING (¼ cup): 50 Cal, 2 g Fat, 0 g Sat Fat, 0 g Trans Fat, 0 mg Chol, 222 mg Sod, 6 g Carb, 2 g Fib, 0 g Prot, 8 mg Calc. **POINTS** value: **1.**

EGGPLANT–BELL PEPPER SPREAD

SILKY RED PEPPER–TOMATO SAUCE ☑

prep 20 MIN   *cook* 15 MIN   *serves* 8

4   red bell peppers
1   garlic clove, chopped
¼   teaspoon salt
2   plum tomatoes, seeded
    and chopped
1   teaspoon red-wine vinegar
1   teaspoon minced fresh
    oregano or ½ teaspoon dried

Pinch black pepper

1 Spray the grill rack with olive oil nonstick spray. Preheat the grill to medium-high or prepare a medium-high fire using the direct method (see page 13).

2 Place the bell peppers on the grill rack and grill, turning frequently, until blackened on all sides, about 15 minutes. Put the peppers in a large zip-close plastic bag and seal the bag: let steam 10 minutes. When cool enough to handle, peel the peppers and remove the seeds; chop the flesh. Set aside.

3 With the side of a large knife, mash the garlic and salt until it forms a paste.

4 Combine the remaining ingredients in a food processor and puree. Add the bell peppers and process until smooth. Pour the tomato mixture through a sieve set over a medium bowl, pressing hard on the solids to extract as much liquid as possible; discard the solids. Serve at once or refrigerate in a covered container up to 1 week or freeze up to 2 months. Spoon over spaghetti, ziti, or penne. Makes 2 cups.

PER SERVING (¼ cup): 19 Cal, 0 g Fat, 0 g Sat Fat, 0 g Trans Fat, 0 mg Chol, 76 mg Sod, 4 g Carb, 1 g Fib, 1 g Prot, 7 mg Calc. **POINTS** value: **0.**

• • •

ORANGE & ONION RELISH ✓

prep 25 MIN   *cook* 30 MIN   *serves* 9

1   red onion, finely chopped

2   large naval oranges, peeled and cut into ½-inch pieces

1   small fennel bulb, trimmed and cut into ½-inch pieces

1   teaspoon capers, drained and minced

¼   teaspoon salt

Pinch cayenne

Chopped fennel fronds (optional)

1 Fill a medium bowl with ice water and add the red onion; let soak about 30 minutes. Drain well in a colander, then pat the onion dry with paper towels.

2 Stir together the onion and all of the remaining ingredients except the fennel fronds in a serving bowl; cover and let stand at room temperature up to 2 hours. Sprinkle with fennel fronds if using. Serve with chicken, turkey, or pork chops. Makes 3 cups.

PER SERVING (⅓ cup): 33 Cal, 0 g Fat, 0 g Sat Fat, 0 g Trans Fat, 0 mg Chol, 88 mg Sod, 8 g Carb, 2 g Fib, 1 g Prot, 32 mg Calc. ***POINTS*** value: **0.**

CLOCKWISE FROM THE LEFT:
FRESH CORN, TOMATO, AND
AVOCADO SALSA,
YELLOW PEPPER & PEACH
SALSA, PAGE 192, AND
SILKY RED PEPPER–TOMATO
SAUCE, PAGE 188

●●●

FRESH CORN, TOMATO & AVOCADO SALSA

prep 20 MIN   *cook* NONE   *serves* 4

1   ear of corn, husk and silk removed

½   ripe Hass avocado, pitted, peeled, and cut into ½-inch pieces

12 grape tomatoes, quartered

3   tablespoons finely chopped red onion

3   fresh basil leaves, very thinly sliced

2   teaspoons olive oil

2   teaspoons lime juice

¼   teaspoon salt

Pinch black pepper

With a knife, remove the kernels from the corn and put in a serving bowl. Add the remaining ingredients and toss to mix well. Serve at once or cover and refrigerate up to 1 day. Makes 1 cup.

PER SERVING (¼ cup): 96 Cal, 6 g Fat, 1 g Sat Fat, 0 g Trans Fat, 0 mg Chol, 157 mg Sod, 11 g Carb, 3 g Fib, 2 g Prot, 11 mg Calc. **POINTS** value: **2.**

• • •

YELLOW PEPPER AND PEACH SALSA ☑

prep 25 MIN   *cook* NONE   *serves* 8

3   small peaches (about
    3 ounces each)

1   yellow bell pepper, cut into
    ¼-inch strips

1   tablespoon chopped
    fresh parsley

2   teaspoons olive oil

1   teaspoon lemon juice

¼   teaspoon salt

⅛   teaspoon ground cumin

⅛   teaspoon cayenne

1 Fill a medium saucepan with water and bring to a boil. Lower the peaches, one at a time, into the water and boil for 30 seconds. With a slotted spoon, transfer the peaches to a cutting board. When cool enough to handle, slip off the peel and remove the pits; cut the peaches into ¼-inch wedges.

2 Gently toss together the peaches and the remaining ingredients in a serving bowl. Serve at once or cover and set aside at room temperature up to 2 hours. Makes 2 cups.

PER SERVING (¼ cup): 26 Cal, 1 g Fat, 0 g Sat Fat, 0 g Trans Fat, 0 mg Chol, 74 mg Sod, 4 g Carb, 1 g Fib, 0 g Prot, 5 mg Calc. **POINTS** value: **0.**

GOOD IDEA

Serve this salsa with Cornish Hens Under a Brick (page 70), Garlic and Herb–Rubbed Turkey (page 107), or Rosemary-Grilled Salmon (page 109).

● ● ●

GRILLED ORANGE & FRESH ROSEMARY CHUTNEY

prep 30 MIN   *cook* 5 MIN   *serves* 6

1	large navel orange, ends cut off
1	garlic clove, chopped
¼	teaspoon salt
1	small red onion, thinly sliced
⅓	cup dried sour cherries or cranberries, chopped
2	teaspoons red-wine vinegar
¼	teaspoon chopped fresh rosemary

Pinch crushed red pepper

1 Spray the grill rack with nonstick spray. Preheat the grill to medium or prepare a medium fire using the direct method (see page 13).

2 Cut half of the orange into ¼-inch slices; set aside. Cut off the peel and white pith from the remaining orange half; cut the flesh into ½-inch pieces; set aside. Place the orange slices on the grill rack and grill, turning, until nicely marked, about 5 minutes. Transfer to a cutting board and coarsely chop; set aside.

3 With the side of a large knife, mash the garlic and salt until it forms a paste.

4 Put the grilled and raw orange, the onion, and garlic paste in a serving bowl. Add the remaining ingredients and toss to mix well. Serve at once or cover and refrigerate up to 2 hours. Makes 1½ cups.

GOOD IDEA

Serve this brightly colored, sweet-tart chutney along with slices of grilled pork tenderloin or skinless, boneless chicken breasts, or with lean lamb chops.

PER SERVING (¼ cup): 43 Cal, 0 g Fat, 0 g Sat Fat, 0 g Trans Fat, 0 mg Chol, 99 mg Sod, 11 g Carb, 2 g Fib, 1 g Prot, 21 mg Calc. **POINTS** value: **0.**

• • •

MEMPHIS DRY RUB

prep 20 MIN   *cook* 2 MIN   *serves* 12

2   garlic cloves, chopped

¼   teaspoon salt

1   tablespoon cumin seeds

¼   cup sweet paprika, preferably Hungarian

2   tablespoons chili powder

2   tablespoons packed brown sugar

1   tablespoon granulated sugar

1 With the side of a large knife, mash the garlic and salt until it forms a paste; set aside.

2 Put the cumin seeds in a small skillet over medium heat. Toast, shaking the pan occasionally, until very fragrant but not burned, 1–2 minutes. Transfer the cumin to a small bowl and let cool completely. In a spice grinder or with a mortar and pestle, finely grind the cumin.

3 Return the ground cumin to the same small bowl. Add the garlic paste and the remaining ingredients; stir until well blended. Use at once or refrigerate in a covered container up to 1 day. Use for spareribs, bone-in chicken breast halves, or pork. Makes about ¾ cup.

PER SERVING (1 tablespoon): 26 Cal, 1 g Fat, 0 g Sat Fat, 0 g Trans Fat, 0 mg Chol, 64 mg Sod, 6 g Carb, 1 g Fib, 1 g Prot, 15 mg Calc. **POINTS** value: **0.**

● ● ●

THAI GREEN CURRY WET RUB

prep 10 MIN *cook* NONE *serves* 6

1 cup light (reduced-fat) coconut milk

2 tablespoons Thai green curry paste

½ teaspoon grated lime zest

2 tablespoons lime juice

Whisk together all the ingredients in a small bowl until smooth. Use at once or refrigerate in a covered container up to 3 days. Use for chicken, lamb, pork or fish. Makes scant 2 cups.

PER SERVING (about 5 tablespoons): 23 Cal, 2 g Fat, 1 g Sat Fat, 0 g Trans Fat, 0 mg Chol, 8 mg Sod, 2 g Carb, 1 g Fib, 1 g Prot, 11 mg Calc. **POINTS** value: **0.**

GOOD IDEA

Intensely flavored and peppery hot, this is a terrific wet rub for chicken, lamb, pork tenderloin, or fish. Chicken and meat can be marinated for as little as 15 minutes.

•••

FENNEL, LEMON & BLACK PEPPER WET RUB ☑

prep 15 MIN   *cook* NONE   *serves* 4

1   garlic clove, chopped
¼   teaspoon salt
1   tablespoon fennel seeds
1½   teaspoons black peppercorns
1   tablespoon grated lemon zest
2   teaspoons lemon juice
2   teaspoons olive oil

1 With the side of a large knife, mash the garlic and salt until it forms a paste; set aside.

2 In a spice grinder or with a mortar and pestle, finely grind the fennel seeds and peppercorns; transfer to a small bowl. Add the garlic paste and the remaining ingredients; stir until mixed well. Use at once or refrigerate in a covered container up to 1 day. Makes ¼ cup.

PER SERVING (1 tablespoon): 29 Cal, 3 g Fat, 0 g Sat Fat, 0 g Trans Fat, 0 mg Chol, 150 mg Sod, 2 g Carb, 1 g Fib, 0 g Prot, 25 mg Calc. **POINTS** value: **1.**

GOOD IDEA
Spread the rub on both sides of 2 (8-ounce) boneless sirloin steaks, trimmed, and grill. Serve with grilled vegetables.

FENNEL, LEMON
& BLACK PEPPER
WET RUB

CLOCKWISE FROM THE LEFT:
SPICY HOISIN MARINADE, PAGE 200
YOGURT-CUMIN MARINADE, PAGE 201, AND
BALSAMIC & FRESH ORANGE MARINADE

●●●

BALSAMIC & FRESH ORANGE MARINADE

prep 10 MIN   *cook* 3 MIN   *serves* 4

2   tablespoons fennel seeds

½   cup balsamic vinegar

½   teaspoon grated orange
       zest

2   tablespoons orange juice

1   tablespoon extra-virgin
       olive oil

¼   teaspoon salt

¼   teaspoon coarsely ground
       black pepper

1 Put the fennel seeds in a medium skillet over medium heat. Toast, stirring frequently, until fragrant and very lightly browned 2–3 minutes. Transfer the fennel seeds to a small bowl and let cool completely.

2 Add the remaining ingredients to the fennel seeds and stir until mixed well. Use at once or refrigerate in a covered container up to 3 days. Use the full recipe to marinate 1 pound of chicken breasts or thighs, pork chops, jumbo shrimp, or swordfish. Makes ¾ cup.

PER SERVING (3 tablespoons): 50 Cal, 4 g Fat, 0 g Sat Fat, 0 g Trans Fat, 0 mg Chol, 152 mg Sod, 3 g Carb, 1 g Fib, 1 g Prot, 39 mg Calc. **POINTS** value: **1.**

GOOD IDEA

For easy clean up, we like to marinate in a zip-close plastic bag. Be sure to squeeze out all the air.

●●●

SPICY HOISIN MARINADE

prep 20 MIN   *cook* 20 MIN   *serves* 8

½ cup reduced-sodium chicken broth

½ cup hoisin sauce

¼ cup unseasoned rice vinegar

4 quarter-size slices peeled fresh ginger, coarsely chopped

3 whole star anise

1 garlic clove, crushed with the side of a large knife

¼ teaspoon crushed red pepper

1 teaspoon Asian (dark) sesame oil

1 Combine all of the ingredients except the sesame oil in a medium heavy saucepan and set over medium-high heat; bring just to a boil. Reduce the heat and barely simmer, whisking frequently, until the mixture is slightly thickened, about 15 minutes.

2 Remove the saucepan from the heat and let cool to room temperature. Pour the marinade through a fine-mesh sieve set over a medium bowl, pressing hard on the solids to extract as much liquid as possible; discard the solids. Whisk in the sesame oil. Use at once or refrigerate in a covered container up to 1 week. Makes 1 cup.

PER SERVING (2 tablespoons): 44 Cal, 1 g Fat, 0 g Sat Fat, 0 g Trans Fat, 0 mg Chol, 294 mg Sod, 7 g Carb, 0 g Fib, 1 g Prot, 8 mg Calc. **POINTS** value: **1.**

GOOD IDEA

The full recipe is the perfect amount for marinating 2 pounds of boneless beef, loin lamb chops, or tuna steaks.

● ● ●

YOGURT-CUMIN MARINADE ☑

prep 15 MIN   *cook* NONE   *serves* 8

1½ cups plain fat-free yogurt

2 tablespoons lemon juice

¾ teaspoon ground cumin

½ teaspoon ground coriander

¼ teaspoon salt

¼ teaspoon black pepper

Stir together all the ingredients in a small bowl. Use at once or refrigerate in a covered container up to 1 week. Use for shrimp, salmon, or chicken. Makes 1½ cups.

PER SERVING (3 tablespoons): 27 Cal, 0 g Fat, 0 g Sat Fat, 0 g Trans Fat, 1 mg Chol, 111 mg Sod, 4 g Carb, 0 g Fib, 3 g Prot, 95 mg Calc. *POINTS* value: **1.**

SWEET THINGS

Chapter 8

•••

GRILLED APRICOT MELBA

prep **15 MIN**   *cook* **20 MIN**   *serves* **4**

¼   cup water

4   tablespoons sugar

1½ cups sweet cherries, pitted

1   teaspoon lemon juice

Pinch cinnamon

4   apricots, halved and pitted

1⅓ cups vanilla low-fat
     frozen yogurt

1 Spray the grill rack with nonstick spray. Preheat the grill to medium or prepare a medium fire using the direct method (see page 13).

2 Meanwhile, combine the water and 2 tablespoons of the sugar in a small saucepan and bring to a boil over medium-high heat. Reduce the heat to low and simmer 2 minutes. Add the cherries and simmer until softened, 5–6 minutes. With a slotted spoon, transfer the cherries to a small bowl; set aside. Continue to cook the juices until syrupy, about 2 minutes longer. Remove the saucepan from the heat and stir in the cherries and lemon juice; set aside.

3 Combine the remaining 2 tablespoons sugar and the cinnamon on a plate. Dip the cut sides of the apricots in the cinnamon sugar. Place the apricots on the grill rack and grill until softened, 2–3 minutes on each side.

4 Place 2 apricot halves in each of 4 dessert dishes and sprinkle with any remaining cinnamon sugar. Add a ⅓-cup scoop of frozen yogurt to each dish and evenly spoon the cherry sauce on top.

PER SERVING (1 apricot Melba): 188 Cal, 2 g Fat, 1 g Sat Fat, 0 g Trans Fat, 5 mg Chol, 52 mg Sod, 41 g Carb, 2 g Fib, 5 g Prot, 142 mg Calc. **POINTS** value: **4**.

●●●

STUFFED CARAMEL PEARS

prep 10 MIN   *cook* 10 MIN   *serves* 4

2   ounces soft (mild) goat cheese, crumbled

2   tablespoons walnuts or pecans, coarsely chopped

1   tablespoon sugar

⅛   teaspoon cinnamon

2   large firm-ripe pears, halved and cored

¼   cup fat-free caramel or butterscotch ice-cream topping

ZAP IT

To speed things up, heat the ice-cream topping in the microwave according to the package directions.

1 Preheat the grill to medium or prepare a medium fire using the direct method (see page 13).

2 Combine the goat cheese, walnuts, sugar, and cinnamon in a small bowl; set aside.

3 Place the pear halves, cut side down, on the grill rack and grill until well marked, about 3 minutes. Transfer the pears, cut side up, to a plate. Spoon the goat cheese mixture evenly into the cavities of the pears. Return the pears to the grill rack, stuffed side up, and grill until a pear is tender when pierced with the tip of a small knife, about 8 minutes.

4 Place a pear half on each of 4 plates. Put the ice-cream topping in a small saucepan and warm over low heat. Drizzle the sauce evenly over the pears.

PER SERVING (1 stuffed pear half and 1 tablespoon topping): 183 Cal, 5 g Fat, 2 g Sat Fat, 0 g Trans Fat, 7 mg Chol, 125 mg Sod, 33 g Carb, 4 g Fib, 4 g Prot, 44 mg Calc. *POINTS* value: **3**.

●●●

TROPICAL PINEAPPLE

prep 10 MIN   *cook* 5 MIN   *serves* 4

2   tablespoons dark rum

¼   teaspoon cinnamon

4   slices peeled and cored
     fresh pineapple

2   tablespoons sugar

2   tablespoons lime juice

2   teaspoons chopped
     fresh cilantro

1   pint mango or passion
     fruit sorbet

2   tablespoons flaked sweetened
     coconut, toasted

1 Combine the rum and cinnamon in a zip-close plastic bag and add the pineapple. Squeeze out the air and seal the bag; turn to coat the pineapple. Let stand at room temperature 1 hour, turning the bag occasionally.

2 Meanwhile, spray the grill rack with nonstick spray. Preheat the grill to medium-high or prepare a medium-high fire using the direct method (see page 13).

3 Combine the sugar, lime juice, and cilantro in a small bowl, stirring until the sugar is dissolved; set aside.

4 Remove the pineapple from rum mixture. Place the pineapple slices on the grill rack and grill until the pineapple is nicely marked, 2–3 minutes on each side.

5 Place a pineapple slice in each of 4 dessert dishes and drizzle with the lime-cilantro syrup. Top each serving with a ½-cup scoop of the sorbet and sprinkle with the coconut. Serve at once.

PER SERVING (1 dish): 224 Cal, 1 g Fat, 1 g Sat Fat, 0 g Trans Fat, 0 mg Chol, 18 mg Sod, 53 g Carb, 2 g Fib, 1 g Prot, 18 mg Calc. ***POINTS*** value: **4.**

• • •

HONEY-PEACH SHORTCAKES

prep 25 MIN   *cook* 20 MIN   *serves* 6

SHORTCAKES

1   cup low-fat buttermilk baking mix

2   tablespoons sugar

2   tablespoons cornmeal

⅓   cup fat-free milk

1   teaspoon grated orange zest

FILLING AND TOPPING

6   peaches, halved and pitted

3   tablespoons + 1 teaspoon honey

2   tablespoons sugar

½   cup thawed frozen fat-free whipped topping

¼   cup plain fat-free Greek-style yogurt

1   tablespoon confectioners' sugar

1 Preheat the oven to 425°F. Spray a baking sheet with nonstick spray.

2 To make the shortcakes, combine the baking mix, sugar, and cornmeal in a medium bowl. Stir together the milk and orange zest in a cup. Add the milk mixture to the cornmeal mixture, stirring until a soft dough forms. On a lightly floured surface, divide the dough into 6 equal pieces and shape each piece into a ball. Press down on each ball to form a disk. Place the disks of dough on the baking sheet and bake until golden brown, about 10 minutes. Let cool on a rack.

3 Meanwhile, spray the grill rack with nonstick spray. Preheat the grill to medium or prepare a medium fire using the direct method (see page 13).

4 To make the fruit filling, brush the cut sides of the peach halves with 1 tablespoon of the honey. Place the peaches, cut side down, on the grill rack and grill until lightly marked and tender, 2–3 minutes on each side. Split the cooled shortcakes and spray the cut sides with nonstick spray. Place on the grill rack and grill, cut side down, until lightly toasted, about 1 minute.

5 Thickly slice the peaches. Put the peaches, sugar, and 2 tablespoons of the honey in a medium bowl and gently stir to combine. Fold together the whipped topping, yogurt, and the remaining 1 teaspoon honey in a small bowl. Place the shortcake bottoms on each of 4 plates. Spoon the peaches evenly on the shortcakes and top with the yogurt mixture. Replace the tops of the shortcakes and dust with the confectioners' sugar.

PER SERVING (1 filled shortcake): 212 Cal, 2 g Fat, 0 g Sat Fat, 0 g Trans Fat, 0 mg Chol, 231 mg Sod, 48 g Carb, 2 g Fib, 4 g Prot, 120 mg Calc. **POINTS** value: **4.**

• • •

GRILLED PEACH-PLUM SORBET

prep 20 MIN   *cook* 15 MIN   *serves* 6

4   peaches (about 5 ounces each), halved and pitted

4   plums (about 3 ounces each), halved and pitted

¾   cup water

½   cup sugar

3   tablespoons honey

1   teaspoon grated lime zest

2   tablespoons lime juice

1 Spray the grill rack with nonstick spray. Preheat the grill to medium or prepare a medium fire using the direct method (see page 13).

2 Spray the cut sides of the peaches and plums with nonstick spray. Place, cut side down, on the grill rack and grill until lightly marked and softened, 2–3 minutes on each side. Put the peaches and plums in a food processor and puree until completely smooth. Set aside.

3 Combine the water and sugar in a medium saucepan and bring to a boil over high heat. Reduce the heat and simmer 5 minutes. Remove the saucepan from the heat and stir in the fruit puree, honey, and lime zest and juice. Pour the mixture through a sieve set over a medium bowl, stirring with a rubber spatula until only skins remain in the sieve; discard the skins. Cover the puree and refrigerate until well chilled, at least 4 hours or up to overnight.

4 Pour the fruit mixture into an ice-cream maker and freeze according to the manufacturer's instructions. Transfer the sorbet to a freezer container and freeze until firm, at least 2 hours or up to 6 hours.

PER SERVING (½ cup): 154 Cal, 1 g Fat, 0 g Sat Fat, 0 g Trans Fat, 0 mg Chol, 2 mg Sod, 37 g Carb, 2 g Fib, 1 g Prot, 9 mg Calc. **POINTS** value: **3.**

HEAVENLY STRAWBERRY SOUFFLÉS

● ● ●

HEAVENLY STRAWBERRY SOUFFLÉS

prep 25 MIN   *cook* 20 MIN   *serves* 6

1   (1-pound) container strawberries, hulled and halved if large

6   tablespoons superfine sugar

2   teaspoons cornstarch

2   teaspoons cold water

¼   cup mixed berry or strawberry preserves

1   teaspoon lemon juice

¼   teaspoon vanilla extract

2   egg whites, at room temperature

Pinch salt

2   tablespoons sliced almonds

1 Spray a vegetable grill topper with nonstick spray. Preheat the grill to medium or prepare a medium fire using the direct method (see page 13).

2 Place the strawberries on the grill topper and place on a grill rack. Grill until softened but not mushy, 2–3 minutes on each side. Let cool about 10 minutes.

3 Combine the strawberries and 2 tablespoons of the sugar in a food processor and process until it forms a chunky puree. Stir together the cornstarch and water in a cup until smooth. Spoon the preserves into a medium saucepan and bring to a simmer over medium heat. Reduce the heat to low and stir in the cornstarch mixture. Cook, stirring constantly, until it thickens and bubbles, about 1 minute. Stir in the strawberry puree. Pour into a medium bowl and stir in the lemon juice and vanilla. Set aside.

4 Meanwhile, preheat the oven to 400°F. Divide ½ cup of the strawberry mixture evenly among 6 (¾-cup) soufflé dishes or custard cups. With an electric mixer on medium speed, beat the egg whites and salt in a large bowl until soft peaks form. Add the remaining 4 tablespoons sugar, 1 tablespoon at a time, beating until stiff, glossy peaks form. Fold the remaining strawberry mixture into the whites.

5 Spoon the meringue mixture into the soufflé dishes dividing it evenly. With a small spoon, swirl the tops of the soufflés to form decorative peaks, then sprinkle evenly with the almonds. Bake the soufflés until risen and lightly browned, 8–10 minutes. Serve at once.

PER SERVING (1 soufflé): 129 Cal, 1 g Fat, 0 g Sat Fat, 0 g Trans Fat, 0 mg Chol, 71 mg Sod, 28 g Carb, 2 g Fib, 2 g Prot, 20 mg Calc. **POINTS** value: **2.**

CINNAMON CORNBREAD WITH RHUBARB-STRAWBERRY COMPOTE

prep 25 MIN *cook* 30 MIN *serves* 8

COMPOTE AND TOPPING

1 pound rhubarb, trimmed and cut into 1-inch pieces

½ cup granulated sugar

½ cup water

1 (1-pound) container strawberries, hulled and halved

1 teaspoon lemon juice

½ cup plain fat-free Greek-style yogurt

1 tablespoon packed brown sugar

CORNBREAD

1¼ cups all-purpose flour

¾ cup cornmeal

¼ cup granulated sugar

2 teaspoons baking powder

1 teaspoon cinnamon

½ teaspoon salt

1 cup fat-free milk

2 tablespoons canola oil

1 large egg

2 tablespoons turbinado sugar

1 To make the compote, combine the rhubarb, sugar, and water in a large saucepan and bring to a boil over medium-high heat. Reduce the heat to low and simmer, partially covered, until the rhubarb is tender but still retains its shape, about 10 minutes. Remove the saucepan from the heat and stir in the strawberries and lemon juice; set aside.

2 To make the topping, combine the yogurt and brown sugar in a small bowl; cover and refrigerate.

3 Preheat the grill to medium or prepare a medium fire using the indirect method (see page 13). When the grill is hot, spray a 10-inch grill-safe skillet with nonstick spray and place on the grill rack on the cooler portion of the grill; preheat 10 minutes.

4 Meanwhile, to make the cornbread, combine the flour, cornmeal, granulated sugar, baking powder, cinnamon, and salt in a large bowl. Beat the milk, oil, and egg in a small bowl. Add the milk mixture to the flour mixture, stirring just until no steaks of flour remain (the batter will be lumpy). Pour the batter into the preheated skillet; sprinkle evenly with the turbinado sugar. Grill, covered, until a toothpick inserted into the center comes out clean, 15–20 minutes, rotating the skillet once. Remove the skillet from the grill and let the cornbread cool in the skillet about 10 minutes.

5 To serve, cut the cornbread into 8 wedges. Place a wedge on each of 8 plates and top evenly with the compote. Spoon the yogurt topping alongside.

PER SERVING (1 wedge cornbread, ⅓ cup fruit compote, and 1 tablespoon yogurt topping): 286 Cal, 5 g Fat, 1 g Sat Fat, 0 g Trans Fat, 27 mg Chol, 305 mg Sod, 56 g Carb, 3 g Fib, 7 g Prot, 242 mg Calc. **POINTS** value: **6.**

● ● ●

GRILLED FRUIT WITH LEMON-GINGER SYRUP

prep 10 MIN   *cook* 15 MIN   *serves* 4

¾ cup water

⅓ cup sugar

1 teaspoon grated lemon zest

1 tablespoon lemon juice

1 teaspoon grated peeled fresh ginger

½ teaspoon fresh thyme leaves

2 nectarines, halved and pitted

2 red plums, halved and pitted

2 apricots, halved and pitted

1 (6-ounce) container raspberries

1 Spray the grill rack with nonstick spray. Preheat the grill to medium or prepare a medium fire using the direct method (see page 13).

2 Combine the water and sugar in a small saucepan and bring to a boil over high heat. Reduce the heat to low and simmer about 3 minutes. Remove the saucepan from the heat and stir in the lemon zest and juice, ginger, and thyme; set aside.

3 Spray the cut sides of the nectarines, plums, and apricots with nonstick spray. Place, cut side down, on the grill rack and grill until the fruit is lightly marked and slightly softened, about 3 minutes on each side. Transfer the fruit to a plate and let cool.

4 Cut the fruit into thick wedges and put in a serving bowl. Pour the lemon-ginger syrup through a sieve set over the fruit. Add the raspberries to the fruit wedges, gently stirring to combine. Cover and refrigerate at least 1 hour or up to 4 hours.

GOOD IDEA

You can vary the fruits for this compote depending on which fruits are ripe and in season. Fresh figs would be a delicious addition, or try grilling some grapes.

PER SERVING (about 1 cup): 87 Cal, 2 g Fat, 0 g Sat Fat, 0 g Trans Fat, 0 mg Chol, 3 mg Sod, 19 g Carb, 5 g Fib, 2 g Prot, 22 mg Calc. **POINTS** value: **1.**

S'MORES BROWNIES

prep 15 MIN   *cook* 40 MIN   *serves* 12

2½ low-fat honey graham crackers

1 (13.7-ounce) box fat-free fudge brownie mix

1 (6-ounce) container plain fat-free yogurt

1 teaspoon vanilla extract

16 marshmallows

¼ cup semisweet chocolate chips

1 Preheat the oven to 350°F. Line an 8-inch square baking pan with foil, allowing the foil to extend over the rim of the pan. Spray with nonstick spray.

2 Break the crackers into rectangles and arrange on the bottom of the pan, cutting the crackers to fit. Prepare the brownie mix according to the package directions using the yogurt and vanilla. Pour the batter over the graham crackers and spread evenly. Bake until a toothpick inserted 1-inch from the edge comes out with crumbs clinging, about 35 minutes; let cool 15 minutes.

3 Meanwhile, preheat the grill to medium-high or prepare a medium-high fire using the direct method (see page 13).

4 Thread 4 marshmallows on each of 4 long metal skewers. Hold 2 skewers just above the grill rack and grill, turning frequently, until the marshmallows are soft and lightly browned in spots, about 2 minutes. With the help of a knife, slide the marshmallows off the skewers and onto the brownies to form a single layer. Repeat with the remaining skewers. While the marshmallows are still warm, spread them over the brownies (the brownies do not have to be completely covered), then sprinkle with the chocolate chips. Return the brownies to the oven and bake until the chocolate chips soften, about 2 minutes. Transfer to a rack and let cool completely.

5 Lift the brownies from the pan using the foil as handles. With a large knife, cut the brownies into 12 equal portions, wiping the knife clean and then holding it under cold running water between cuts.

PER SERVING (1 brownie): 190 Cal, 2 g Fat, 1 g Sat Fat, 0 g Trans Fat, 0 mg Chol, 167 mg Sod, 42 g Carb, 0 g Fib, 4 g Prot, 56 mg Calc. **POINTS** value: **4.**

S'MORES BROWNIES

• • •

BANANA TURTLE NAPOLEONS

prep 10 MIN   *cook* 10 MIN   *serves* 4

2 unpeeled firm-ripe bananas, halved lengthwise

1 tablespoon packed brown sugar

4 frozen low-fat seven-grain waffles, thawed

1 cup dulche de leche low-fat frozen yogurt

3 tablespoons fat-free hot fudge sauce, heated

1 tablespoon finely chopped salted peanuts

HOW WE DID IT
Leaving the peel on the bananas while grilling helps to hold them together as they soften and decreases the likelihood of their sticking to the grill.

1 Spray the grill rack with nonstick spray. Preheat the grill to medium or prepare a medium fire using the direct method (see page 13).

2 Sprinkle the cut sides of the bananas with the brown sugar; let stand about 10 minutes. Place the bananas, cut side down, on the grill rack and grill until caramelized, about 2 minutes. Turn and grill until the bananas are tender and the skins begin to separate from the flesh, 4–5 minutes longer. Just before the bananas are done, place the waffles on the grill rack and grill until hot and lightly marked, about 1 minute on each side.

3 Cut the waffles in half; place one half on each of 4 dessert plates. Peel the banana halves and cut crosswise in half. Top each waffle half with a ¼-cup scoop of the frozen yogurt, spreading it to cover the waffle. Place 2 pieces of banana on top of each serving, then cover with the remaining waffle halves. Drizzle evenly with the hot fudge sauce and sprinkle with the peanuts. Serve at once.

PER SERVING (1 napoleon): 272 Cal, 4 g Fat, 1 g Sat Fat, 0 g Trans Fat, 4 mg Chol, 248 mg Sod, 56 g Carb, 5 g Fib, 9 g Prot, 153 mg Calc. **POINTS** value: **5**.

VIETNAMESE BEEF AND
NOODLE SALAD, PAGE 49

DRY AND LIQUID MEASUREMENT EQUIVALENTS

If you are converting the recipes in this book to metric measurements, use the following chart as a guide.

TEASPOONS	TABLESPOONS	CUPS	FLUID OUNCES
3 teaspoons	1 tablespoon		½ fluid ounce
6 teaspoons	2 tablespoons	⅛ cup	1 fluid ounce
8 teaspoons	2 tablespoons plus 2 teaspoons	⅙ cup	
12 teaspoons	4 tablespoons	¼ cup	2 fluid ounces
15 teaspoons	5 tablespoons	⅓ cup minus 1 teaspoon	
16 teaspoons	5 tablespoons plus 1 teaspoon	⅓ cup	
18 teaspoons	6 tablespoons	¼ cup plus 2 tablespoons	3 fluid ounces
24 teaspoons	8 tablespoons	½ cup	4 fluid ounces
30 teaspoons	10 tablespoons	½ cup plus 2 tablespoons	5 fluid ounces
32 teaspoons	10 tablespoons plus 2 teaspoons	⅔ cup	
36 teaspoons	12 tablespoons	¾ cup	6 fluid ounces
42 teaspoons	14 tablespoons	1 cup minus 2 tablespoons	7 fluid ounces
45 teaspoons	15 tablespoons	1 cup minus 1 tablespoon	
48 teaspoons	16 tablespoons	1 cup	8 fluid ounces

VOLUME	
¼ teaspoon	1 milliliter
½ teaspoon	2 milliliters
1 teaspoon	5 milliliters
1 tablespoon	15 milliliters
2 tablespoons	30 milliliters
3 tablespoons	45 milliliters
¼ cup	60 milliliters
⅓ cup	80 milliliters
½ cup	120 milliliters
⅔ cup	160 milliliters
¾ cup	175 milliliters
1 cup	240 milliliters
1 quart	950 milliliters

LENGTH

1 inch	25 millimeters
1 inch	2.5 centimeters

OVEN TEMPERATURE

250°F	120°C	400°F	200°C
275°F	140°C	425°F	220°C
300°F	150°C	450°F	230°C
325°F	160°C	475°F	250°C
350°F	180°C	500°F	260°C
375°F	190°C	525°F	270°C

WEIGHT

1 ounce	30 grams
¼ pound	120 grams
½ pound	240 grams
1 pound	480 grams

NOTE: Measurement of less than ⅛ teaspoon is considered a dash or a pinch. Metric volume measurements are approximate.

RECICPE INDEX

POINTS VALUE RECIPE INDEX

Jerk Red Snapper with Pineapple, 111

Mexican Grilled Corn, 142

Polenta with Rosemary-Garlic Mushrooms, 149

Roasted Corn & Chive Soup, 37

Scallops with Tomato-Onion Salsa, 114

Stuffed Caramel Pears, 206

Tilapia with Tomato-Orange Sauce, 131

Tofu & Apple Salad with Pomegranate Vinaigrette, 84

Lemongrass Pork Patties with Asian Carrot-Apple Salad, 57

Pastrami-Style Flank Steak, 43

Rosemary Chicken with Butternut Squash & Apples, 123

S'Mores Brownies, 214

Spicy Linguine with Grilled Shrimp & Clams, 80

Tropical Pineapple, 207

Turkey Tostadas with Smoky Tomatillo Salsa, 71

Vietnamese Beef & Noodle Salad, 49

Paella Salad with Chicken & Shrimp Skewers, 104

Pork Tenderloin with Autumn Fruit, 120

Red Onion & Goat Cheese Pizza, 170

Saltimbocca Rolls with Grilled Artichokes, 51

Salmon with Tomato-Olive Sauce, 128

Spaghetti with Shrimp, Tomatoes & Peas, 178

Tuna with Mango-Strawberry Salad, 76

4 POINTS value

Asian-Style Halibut with Pea Shoot Salad, 79

Asian-Style Spareribs with Ginger Dipping Sauce, 95

Beef Brisket with Feta Chimichurri Sauce, 91

Best-Ever Lemon-Roasted Chicken, 62

Chicken Breasts Stuffed with Herbed Goat Cheese, 59

Chicken with Spinach & Tomatoes, 125

Chili-Rubbed Beef Tenderloin with Chunky Pico de Gallo, 88

Cod with Salsa Cruda, 78

Garlicky Eggplant & Tempeh Stir-fry, 85

Grilled Apricot Melba, 204

Honey-Peach Shortcakes, 208

Jerk Pork with Curried Pineapple Salsa, 50

5 POINTS value

All-American BBQ Chicken, 102

Balsamic-Glazed Flank Steak with Arugula, 42

Banana Turtle Napoleons, 216

Chili-Rubbed Turkey Breast, 105

Cornish Hens Under a Brick, 70

Grilled Lamb Kofta, 101

Grilled Pork, Orange, & Red Onion Salad, 94

Grilled Sausage & Pepper Heroes, 171

Mediterranean-Style Mixed Seafood Grill, 81

Mojito-Barbecued Chicken, 65

Moroccan-Style Chicken with Olives, 69

Orange & Rosemary-Rubbed Pork Chops with Nectarines, 54

6 POINTS value

Asian-Style Beef & Lettuce Packages, 90

Chicken with Orange & Basil Gremolata, 99

Chicken Satay with Red Curry-Peanut Sauce, 67

Cinnamon Cornbread with Rhubarb-Strawberry Compote, 212

Cornmeal-Crusted Chicken with Corn-Tomato Ragout, 66

Filet Mignon with Apricot-Orange Sauce, 118

Greek-Style Chicken with Cucumber-Yogurt Sauce, 126

Grilled Kielbasa with Caraway Cabbage, 72

Hoisin Pork Burgers with Asian-Style Salad, 122

Individual Meat Loaves with Peppers & Sun-Dried Tomatoes, 119

Maple-Brined Pork Chops with Basil-Stuffed Nectarines, 96

NOTES